UNSPEAKABLE

THE TRUTH ABOUT GRIEF

Printed in the United States of America

First Edition 10 9 8 7 6 5 4 3 2 1

CIP DATA pending

ISBN: 1-886298-14-9
LCCN: 2002103212

Bayou Publishing
2524 Nottingham
Houston, TX 77005-1412
Ph: (713) 526-4558
Fax: 713-526-4342
http://www.BayouPublishing.com

UNSPEAKABLE

THE TRUTH ABOUT GRIEF

Herb Orrell

Bayou Publishing

HOUSTON, TEXAS

*This book is dedicated to my wife Bethe
and my children Jason and Rachael*

"Suffering isn't ennobling, recovery is."

—*Christian N. Barnard*

Acknowledgments

My deepest heartfelt thanks to my mother Dorothy Orrell for her love and care and belief in me, and to my late father Herbert M. Orrell Sr., for his guidance and inspiration.

I owe a great debt of gratitude to the New Mexico Annual Conference of the United Methodist Church for allowing me to serve the following congregations: Lordsburg UMC, Genesis UMC, Trinity UMC, Vista Ysletta, Epworth UMC, and Tobin Park UMC. In each of these congregations I received an enormous amount of grace and love. I am deeply thankful to the people who inspired and challenged me to grow and learn.

George and Janis Shoup, Brad and Peg Herndon, Dr. Leonard Gillingham, Rev. Charles Crutchfield, Rev. Chuck Little, Rev. Ellen Little, Dr. Harold Brach, Dr. Marian Poindexter, Dr. Peter White, Mary Vachris, Rev. Dennis Hawk, Bill and Ted Hoppe, Edith and Ted White, Miriam Gaffney, Bill Anderson, The Wing and a Prayer Gospel

Band, Dottie Lollicker, Melissa Olander, Tom and Toni Seward, Paul and Connie Jennings, Nora Heather, Larry and Rosetta Springer, David Warren, Richard Puckett, Judi Bard, Barbara Shepherd, the staff at Dr. Sanford's oncological clinic who have taken such loving care of my daughter Rachael.

Dr. Bill Kerley for his advice on this manuscript, my editors, Judy King, Deborah Shelton, and Roger Leslie, and my publisher, Dr. Victor Loos who recognized the potential of this project and assembled a "dream team" of professionals to ensure this book would reach those who need it.

Contents

CHAPTER 1

The Hidden Stage in the Grieving Process

> Even at his most powerless, man's existence is
> never without meaning.
>
> —*Suikoden*

In her 1969 book, *On Death and Dying*, Dr. Elisabeth Kübler-Ross introduced a ground-breaking idea. Grief is a process involving six necessary and predictable stages: denial, anger, bargaining, depression, and acceptance. Given sufficient time and care, one stage of the grieving process gradually melts into the next, culminating finally in some measure of peaceful acceptance and hope for the future.

Two generations of doctors, therapists, and clergy have echoed the teachings of Kübler-Ross, encouraging those who grieve to work the process. At this very moment untold numbers of people who have experienced trauma—

loss of a loved one, incest, rape, natural disasters, among other possibilities—are clinging to this promise.

If working this process is truly the road to recovery, and acceptance and hope wait to embrace us at the end of the grieving process, why do so many people never reach that final, emancipating stage? Grief becomes a permanent part of so many people's lives because Kübler-Ross's process is fundamentally flawed. Perhaps we've missed the flaw for more than 30 years because it's so obvious.

The Fundamental Flaw

The first four stages of the grieving process—denial, anger, bargaining and depression—make perfect sense. But can we really entrust our recovery to the notion that depression will somehow lead to acceptance?

Even mild forms of depression can bring all kinds of crippling symptoms—intense feelings of sadness, dejection, emptiness, irritability, hopelessness, exhaustion, difficulty sleeping, headaches, back pains, and gastrointestinal upset.

The 60 million prescriptions written each year in this country for anti-depressants are ample evidence that depression is not in the habit of resolving itself—much less helping a trauma victim unlock the door to acceptance and recovery.

The Search for Meaning

The grieving process, in fact, includes another critical stage: the search for meaning.

At some point following a trauma, we will come to conclusions about the meaning of the event. Whether our search for meaning begins at the moment of impact or years later, the questions we must answer are enormously difficult: Why did it happen? What does it say about me, about life? And, for many of us, how can my suffering be reconciled with my belief in a just and loving God?

Why do we look for meaning in trauma? The simple answer is that human beings look for meaning in everything.

Even the most mundane, ordinary occurrences can fill us with questions: Why didn't the boss say "good morning" when I walked past her? Why did my daughter laugh when I asked her about her boyfriend? Why did the waitress give me that look? What does it *mean*?

Often we find more meaning in what didn't happen, what wasn't said. By the time we take our first baby steps, we have already developed an acute sensitivity to subtle inferences we might detect in a gesture, the flutter of an eyelash, a tone of voice, or the quiver of a lip.

Whether our search for meaning is the result of a neurological imperative, cultural training, or our chosen spiritual path, you and I work hard at it all day long.

If we feel compelled to find meaning in the mundane moments of our lives, how much more important is it for us to find meaning in the most traumatic events of our lives?

The Purpose of Meaning

Meaning plays a critical role in recovery. If we finally manage to move on to acceptance, it is not because depression leads us there; it is because we find some meaning for our suffering that allows us to accept it and go on.

So the question becomes, what meaning can we possibly find in our suffering to help us accept what has happened and find peace and hope for the future? When my child is diagnosed with leukemia; when an accident at work confines me to a wheelchair; when psychological, sexual, or physical abuse has scarred me for life; when half the members of the third-grade class are mowed down in the schoolyard by a madman's automatic weapon; when an earthquake, plane crash, flood, drunk driver, or terrorist bomb takes away my loved ones in the blink of an eye, what explanation, what meaning can I cling to that will help me survive?

Throughout history, philosophers, theologians, poets, prophets, playwrights, novelists, and many others have wrestled with these questions, each offering advice as to what meaning we *should* find in our suffering.

But what if we could look into this very private process and discover the meanings that people actually cling to when they suffer?

Scientists engaged in post traumatic stress disorder (PTSD) research have done just that—uncovered the meaning people find in their suffering. And the results are startling.

Window to the Soul: *What PTSD Research Tells Us About the Grieving Process*

The symptoms of PTSD have been described in literature as far back as ancient Greece, but it wasn't until the end of WWII that researchers had an opportunity to study the long-term effects of trauma in a controlled environment.

Thousands of returning soldiers (most of whom had never been hit by bullets or shrapnel) were experiencing a variety of debilitating symptoms including denial, emotional numbing, anger, rage, rushes of anxiety, sadness, fear, confusion, difficulty sleeping, stomach upset, loss of appetite, and in some cases hallucinations. Simple exposure to the trauma of war had, on its own, produced serious emotional and physical problems.

When the results of this early research into the effects of trauma were published, something happened that no one could have predicted. Doctors across the country reported seeing the same symptoms, in varying degrees of severity, in patients suffering from very different kinds of traumas. Somewhere in this scramble to make sense of it all, the term PTSD was born.

Not everything we have learned in 50 years of PTSD research is directly applicable to all those who grieve. Some of the breakthroughs are purely medical in nature, such as advanced treatments for depression and specialized therapeutic strategies which are best left for the most severe cases of trauma. However, a number of discoveries provide remarkable insights into the grieving process.

Trauma is far more pervasive than we ever realized. For years the term "trauma" was used only to describe exposure to a life-threatening experience. But recent studies reveal that PTSD symptoms can be caused by many events: death of a loved one; physical, sexual or psychological abuse; betrayal by a trusted person or institution; natural disasters; acute illness; terrorism; industrial accidents; prolonged unemployment; even divorce can produce PTSD symptoms in both parents and children.

You don't *have to experience trauma directly to suffer PTSD symptoms.* When trauma strikes a loved one—a spouse, child, parent, friend—we can suffer the same or greater symptoms as the victim.

If we factor in the duration of the grieving process with the knowledge that everyone who experiences trauma directly or indirectly will grieve, the number of people dealing with some significant level of grief at any one time must be incalculable.

It is in the area of meaning, however, that PTSD research has made what may prove to be its most remarkable discovery. Based on the long-term study of thousands of PTSD victims, researchers have learned that **all trauma victims search for meaning and they all come to the same conclusion.**

The Question that Changes the World

While the extent of bodily harm, economic loss, or PTSD symptoms vary with circumstance, researchers have identified one component found in virtually all traumatic events, that transcends ethnic, economic, educational, or even religious differences. Trauma victims ask, "Why me?" and in the attempt to make sense of their suffering, *they blame themselves for the traumatic event.*

Perhaps even more than the trauma itself, it is this question that changes us. Whether we shout it from the rooftops, whisper it under our breath, or wonder about it so privately deep within us that we don't even hear ourselves, once we ask "Why me?" we are never the same.

Why would a rape or incest victim blame herself for the abuse? Why would a mother wonder, "What did I do to deserve this?" as her son's casket is lowered into the ground? Why would someone throw common sense to the wind and conclude that the hurricane, earthquake, or car wreck must be punishment for some sin or character flaw? Why don't we stand up and fight for our innocence?

Why We Blame Ourselves for Trauma

What possible value could self-blame have in the process of recovering from trauma? Dr. Melvin Learner, a crime victim psychologist at the University of Waterloo, answers that question this way: "People believe that they live in a *Just World* and they will do almost anything to protect that belief."

When we understand the preeminent position the Just World belief has held in our collective consciousness throughout the ages, it begins to make sense why most of us feel there is no price too great to protect it—even denying our own innocence.

The idea of a Just World (known to most of us by the familiar saying, "You reap what you sow") is among the most ancient of all beliefs. It has influenced social mythologies, judicial systems, and religions as far back as the Code of Hammurabi (circa 4000 BC).

At a personal level, believing there's a fundamental order and fairness at work in the world provides people an emotional infrastructure that gives life meaning. Seeing a direct cause-and-effect relationship between choices and results creates a sense of stability and personal safety.

The Just World belief has had enormous influence on human spirituality. Because our understanding of love is so closely connected to ideas of fairness, predictability, and trust, the assurance that we live in a Just World has long been a necessary prerequisite for faith in a loving God.

Part of the attraction of this belief is its simple logic: good choices bring safety and spiritual wholeness, bad choices bring danger and separation from God. This apparent simplicity, however, is deceptive.

"You reap what you sow" is an all-or-nothing proposition that must be applied to each of life's circumstances or it cannot be applied at all. Selective application will, in time, cause the system to crumble.

Victims can maintain their innocence by accepting that a traumatic event was unjust or undeserved. In the process, however, they must relinquish rights to a Just World belief system and, by default, any faith they might have had in a loving God.

In addition to any philosophical or theological implications, accepting blame for trauma has numerous practical advantages. The most basic is damage control. If it is true that we can bring trauma upon ourselves, then we should be able to take appropriate actions to prevent trauma from recurring in the future.

Taking personal responsibility for trauma makes the event smaller and more manageable—it cuts the problem down to size. If suffering is seen as a legitimate by-product of a personal failure rather than evidence of a system failure, it is far less catastrophic. Although we may have incurred physical, economic, and psychological devastation, our belief in a Just World, safe universe, and a loving God can remain intact.

You can fight for your innocence if you must. Go ahead; make a fist and scream at the heavens. But be aware of the consequences. No one will stand by your side, no one will fight with you. There are no religious beliefs in this world that will welcome and support your innocence, no sacred rituals or ceremonies, no mythology or traditions to lean on. Even if you prove beyond a shadow of a doubt that your suffering is unearned, you are left with only one chilling conclusion: Regardless of your behavior, this Unjust World leaves you vulnerable to unpredictable, meaningless and random violence. That thought is usually more than the human heart can bear.

What takes place then, in the depths of the grieving process, is a kind of brass-knuckles back room plea-bargaining. Faced with the impossible task of not only *defending* our innocence, but also *living* with our innocence, we plead guilty hoping to receive a reduced sentence.

This last reason may be the most important one of all. The self-blame strategy can do much more than just get us functioning again. Blaming ourselves for trauma can actually make us a "better person."

The search for meaning begins with a rigorous moral inventory. We comb through every shadowy corner of our lives, our thoughts, our dark secrets in an effort to identify the root cause, that one particular sin or character flaw for which we are being punished.

After we determine the root cause (there's always something to pin it on), we then set out to change it. But we don't stop there. Driven by fear of recurring trauma, we launch a self-improvement campaign. We look for ways to be more ethical and honest and caring, or to become a better parent, spouse, friend, worker, and churchgoer. "Hard times make us stronger" is not just a sentimental needlepoint hanging over a cozy fireplace. It can really happen.

Self-blame doesn't overtake us without a struggle. We don't blame ourselves easily, and we seldom do it out loud. It is a deeply personal and private decision—the "hidden" stage in the grieving process. In the end, however, we accept blame for our suffering because it is the most effective strategy we have for protecting what is really important to us.

Why the Grieving Never Ends

We don't realize at first that taking blame for trauma is risky business. The recovery process we sign up for turns out to be a kind of delicate high-wire act. At the end of the wire the faint outline of our new life waits to embrace us. Getting there is a question of balance.

There are many slippery spots on this narrow wire. Fear, uncertainty, sadness, loneliness, and depression can make us lose our footing. But the most difficult adjustments of all are the doubts.

Invariably we will second-guess our decision. Although we have confessed our guilt, we may not be completely convinced of it. There will be haunting reminders that we made this agreement in the heat of battle, under extreme duress. Was it really our own free decision? Or was it a forced confession, a conditional surrender, an act of malicious compliance? Did the punishment fit the crime?

Just when we think we might be getting better, a sound, a stranger's face, a picture in a magazine—any of a thousand insignificant, unrelated triggers—can launch us into fits of anger, anxiety, or depression. Memory is often our worst enemy. It holds us hostage to the past, mercilessly replaying the event over and over again, making us relive every bitter detail.

Sooner or later we fall. Even the most dedicated and determined among us eventually caves in to the relentless pressures of sustaining this strategy day after day, year after year. It is only when we fall, however, that the real secret to this grieving process is revealed.

Stretched out beneath us has always been a tightly woven safety net of reassuring cultural attitudes, beliefs, and traditions; a vast array of Just World stories, myths, and folklore; and well-trodden spiritual paths of reconciliation and new birth based on confession and forgiveness. When our best efforts finally give out, we fall into the arms of a world that supports and defends our decision and helps us get back on the wire again. With this safety net below us, we never fall too far or too hard, and the balancing act can begin again, and again.

Over the years this safety net has faced many challenges. Science changed the shape of the earth and moved the sun to the center of our galaxy. Anthropologists found apes in our family tree. Priests and theologians questioned the divinity of Christ. Philosophers announced that God is dead.

Through these and countless other storms, the Just World belief persevered, faithfully fashioning for each successive generation a belief system in which every event had meaning and purpose, in which life itself was a kind of classroom offering us a series of carefully tailored individual lessons taught by a benevolent and loving God. The hope of trauma recovery was available to anyone, at a price most would pay.

The reason our grieving never seems to end is that the safety net we have depended upon for ages is coming apart at the seams.

Falling Through the Net

Years from now it will be the task of historians to try and explain why this ancient safety net finally came undone. When they do, surely a couple of factors will top the list.

When instant communication put us anywhere on the planet in a heartbeat, we were confronted for the first time by the amount of trauma in this world—the sheer numbers of people who suffer droughts, famines, disease, terrorism, poverty, natural disasters. Could we continue indefinitely to convince ourselves that each one of these events was punishment for someone's bad behavior?

The psychology of personality development made it abundantly clear that the basic building block of mental health is the ability to make appropriate distinctions between what is and isn't our responsibility. Taking blame for trauma in order to feel better as quickly as possible and to protect our belief in a Just World and loving God isn't the noble or courageous thing to do. It isn't even an expression of religious faithfulness. It's an act of self-betrayal that can have profound consequences down the road.

Archaeological research revealed that long before Homo sapiens arrived on the scene, this planet was already a very hostile place. While you and I may be able to improve our chances at safety and security by our adaptations, inventions, and behavior, there will always be a degree of inherent danger in this world beyond our control that has nothing to do with the choices we make.

These and many other factors worked together to create an ever-increasing mountain of evidence that confirmed our worst nightmare: This is not a Just World we are living in, no matter how desperately we wish it were so.

The solution then should be obvious. We will refuse to blame ourselves for trauma and never get up on that high wire again. Ironically, as sensible as that may sound, it is not an option.

Blaming ourselves for trauma is not any more "voluntary" than any of the other stages of grief. In fact, this strategy is so deeply ingrained within us that it may actually be a kind of evolutionary adaptation carved inextricably into our subconscious—more of an instinct than a decision, a survival "plan B" for the inevitable times when fight or flight fails us.

On the surface things will continue to look much the same as they always have. Life will bring trauma; people will grieve. Following in the footsteps of those before us, we will blame ourselves for what we have suffered, step out on the recovery high wire, and try our best to maintain some kind of balance. Sooner or later we will fall. Only the results will be different.

Falling through the safety net is a shattering experience that forces us to face some very difficult truths. Our survival strategy has failed us. The terrible confession we made at gunpoint didn't save us after all. The plea-bargain wasn't just a little sleight of hand; it was a profound act of self-betrayal. For all our efforts, we are no different from the spouse who takes blame for everything in a marriage in order to keep the peace or the incest victim who maintains the public appearance of a relationship for the sake of survival. We have pawned our innocence and all we're left with is a secret, unspeakable, burning rage.

America's Great Spiritual Quest?

On August 17, 1998, an earthquake measuring 7.4 on the Richter scale devastated northwestern Turkey killing more than 17,000 people and leaving hundreds of thousands homeless. In the aftermath of this disaster, a different kind of story overshadowed familiar tales of heroism and self-sacrifice. Its message bears repeating.

One day, a scientist brought chilling news to a small mountainside village. "Your homes are located directly on a fault line," he warned. "You're in grave danger." The elders called a meeting to devise a plan that would save the town. Following a great deal of discussion, they voted unanimously to move the fault line.

On the subject of grief, our "elders" are no different. Everywhere around us evidence confirms that our strategy for grief recovery doesn't work. Yet as increasing numbers of people find it impossible to resolve their grief, our caregivers, clergy, and doctors keep repeating the same message: *Time heals all wounds; work the process.*

With this mindset, we blame ourselves not only for suffering, but also for not getting better. We think we didn't try hard enough, or we weren't patient enough. So we try journaling, support groups, forgiveness, therapy, medication—all of which might soften the symptoms of grief, but bring no real resolution.

The grieving process is becoming a business as big and self-perpetuating and ineffective as the diet industry. We are led to believe that if we only hear the same message a different way—from let's say the perspective of a grandmother, sibling, husband, wife, son, daughter, or best of all, a celebrity—maybe *this* time we'll finally get it, the process will work, and we'll get on with our lives again.

Angry, lost, and empty, we drift from one guru or spiritual gimmick to another. What the media call "America's great spiritual quest" is more appropriately America's great spiritual famine. We're more hungrier and more desperate than ever, we're not getting any lasting answers, and we're quickly running out of options. In our wandering we've come up short. We've pushed as hard as we can on that fault line, but it hasn't moved an inch.

Then where is the hope for the future?

Making Peace with Our Innocence

The task for us who grieve today is really no different than it has ever been. The fundamental issue to be resolved in trauma has always been and always will be our innocence.

Falling through the net into this uncharted territory has one advantage: We come face to face with our innocence again, and we have one more chance to make things right.

Perhaps our poets, artists, and visionaries have already entered this uncharted territory and are preparing a place for us. One day philosophers may articulate these truths so clearly that we'll enshrine them in museums, record them in operas, make them the themes of great novels and sonnets.

We can only pray that the custodians of our great faiths will awaken from their deathlike sleep and find the courage to send their prophets into this new land. One day those who stand in the pulpits—from the greatest urban cathedrals to the most humble country chapels—will show by the stories falling from their lips a new understanding: *those in their care seek salvation not only from their guilt, but also from their innocence.*

The real pioneer into this new land will be the everyday person on the street, the woman next door, the face in the mirror—the individual hungering for the kind of truth that speaks to everyday experiences. The truth that pioneering person seeks is one that helps make it through the night, keeps brittle marriages from falling to pieces, raises responsible children, or reclaims the inalienable human right of being able to live again after trauma has put a knife through the heart.

In the pages ahead you will find no creed, no philosophy, just the story of one person who journeyed into that uncharted territory and, by the grace of God, finally found the peace he was looking for.

CHAPTER 2	*Learning to Pretend*

> I not only have my secrets, I am my secrets. And
> you are your secrets. Our trusting each other
> enough to share them has much to do with the
> secret of what it means to be human.
>
> —*Frederick Buechner*

The merciless Mexican sun, having scorched a path through the heart of another August day, finally settled down on a golden bed of softness. A blanket of dreamy violet mist rose off the salty cove and melted into the dark distance. Staring out across the endless ocean, I remembered my secret.

Down the road from our bungalow, the cantinas were coming to life. As soon sunburned tourists began numbing themselves in rivers of mariachis, tequila, Corona, and lime, I stared across the endless Pacific seeking a more natural peace. Instead, I remembered my secret. It was killing me. One last night in this bewitching fishing village and, in the morning, we would head back home.

The secret was killing me, as secrets often do. My wife recognized the death in my eyes but she was either too frightened to say anything or I was too lost to listen. Anyway, our words didn't penetrate in those days. Instead they fell lifeless to the ground like sparrows into a windowpane.

My congregation didn't know. Each Sunday morning as the gentle tide of one more worship service washed over them, the message floating on the surface must have seemed just thoughtful enough, and predictable enough, to reassure them of my vital signs. But underneath the smile, the sermons, the benedictions, and the prayers, underneath the waves, I was drowning.

As the sun disappeared beneath the vast horizon, I thought of my father lying in his hospice bed, and I began to weep. First it was the Alzheimer's disease, then the lung infection, then what everyone surmised was a self-imposed starvation. Once or twice a month I would make the three-hundred-mile trip to visit him. I hoped each visit would be my last.

All my life he had been so good to me. He had a wonderful heart and a great mind. He was always more than willing to lavish his endless patience on my wild fantasies and burning questions.

He would rather have been paralyzed than made to suffer the indignities of losing his mind. For years he had been a teacher, and his students, never getting enough in the classroom, would often flock to our house on the week-ends. I hated having to share him with so many other seekers. I loved it, too.

Then his mind started to go, and he could be found most of the time standing in front of the living room mirror—a wrinkled patchwork of mismatched plaid drooping from his coat-hanger body—lecturing to a classroom of students who were no longer there; staring blankly into the mirror, vomiting up strings of word nonsense. A clown with a pie in his face.

"Come on, Dad, it's time to eat."

"What day is this?" he'd ask, again.

During those early days of grieving I was often visited by waves of childhood memories. Sometimes they were reminders of things I wished I had done differently, or not at all—ways in which I had failed myself and those who loved me. If only I had tried harder, been better. If only I had said the right thing; if only....

There were other memories too, ones that gave me the strange feeling that there was something familiar about my grief, that in some unexplainable way what I was feeling might have actually begun many years earlier.

I remembered peering through the safety of my mostly uneventful childhood and noticing that things would happen to people—innocent people—that should never have happened. There was a boy named Jimmy McDonald in my second grade class who was "different," so he was made to suffer endless indignities at the hands of his classmates.

There was Artie, our gnarled little neighbor who rolled his wheelchair up and down the sidewalk in front of my house each day. He told all the kids that he got that way because he didn't eat his vegetables—but the look in his eyes was so fiercely at odds with the laughter on his lips.

There was the butcher next door who, after drinking all weekend, would take out his fear and anger on his family, the cries of his victims piercing the night air past my window.

Like many other families in our working class neighborhood, *Life* was a permanent fixture on the living room coffee table. I loved the rivers of intoxicating optimism that poured from its pages. "The world is a wonderful place," said the pictures, "just look and see." With the lush pictorials of Mt. Rushmore, the Grand Canyon, or Mickey Mantle hitting a World Series home run cradled safely in my arms, I would dream the big dreams of the blessed.

One day, however, I got a rude awakening. The mail came and in the bundle of letters and circulars was the familiar brown paper that guarded our latest issue of *Life Magazine*. I ripped off the wrapping and staring back at me from the cover were the hollow faces and mutilated bodies of thalidomide children.

On Sunday mornings I was made to stuff myself into my little boy suit so I could be properly dragged off to church. Early on, I wanted to believe that the church would be a place where I could find some answers—the breathless quiet of the sanctuary when we prayed; the shattering power of the pipe organ; the magical glow of the candles;

gold leaf accents on mahogany wood carvings; the c/ shrouded in black on Good Friday; the dazzling, blin/ whiteness of Easter Sunday—all of this made me think the church would be a safe place for my burning questions.

The days of hellfire and brimstone had pretty much run their course and what we heard instead was more about God's love. "God loves you" said the minister, "more than you can imagine; no matter what you do." In fact, "God loves you so much He sent His son to die for your sins. Believe this and you will go to heaven."

This arrangement was quite appealing to me. I found comfort imagine a benevolent, merciful Creator whose job it was to take care of me, guide me, and befriend me. But the more I listened, the more unsettling it became.

I remember one morning in particular. Our Sunday School class had practiced week after week for an Easter program. Boys in white shirts, girls in starched dresses, we stood frozen before the congregation and sang, "Jesus Loves Me." Suddenly the sea of proud parents in the pews faded away and I saw instead the look of bitter loneliness that swept across Jimmy's face when children made fun of him. I saw Artie the paraplegic dutifully wheeling himself back home after we decided that the novelty of his afflic- tion was no longer amusing. I saw the black and blue bruises on my friend's face and arms when a week later he was finally allowed out to play. It made me wonder, *Does Jesus love them, too?*

What I knew about love seemed so much different from God's love. To me, love was the cool cloth in my mother's hand as she wiped the fever from my brow. It was the wildly colorful yarns my father and I would spin on our nightly walks through the neighborhood. Love was the patient look in my grandmother's eyes as she listened to my hopes and dreams and filled me with too-sweet milky tea.

As imperfect as we were, at least we knew what love was for. Love was there to ease the pain, to right what was wrong. Love was fair, dependable, predictable. Love protected us, rescued us, risked for us, sacrificed for us. And then love was something we returned because we wanted to, needed to. Above all, love was never silent to the suffering of another.

The love I knew, the love I hungered for, was not only different from, but also far better than, God's love. If the Creator of our world really loved us, I thought, Artie wouldn't be in that wheelchair. Alex would never have to cringe beneath his father's belt again.

I made the mistake of sharing my doubts with others in our church. I was scolded by the minister, who told me I was showing a lack of faith. My Sunday School teacher looked so bewildered when I asked her, "If God loves us so much, why does He let us suffer?"

"God works in mysterious ways," she answered in the way you might excuse yourself when your stomach growls.

I was made to feel that I had witnessed something I shouldn't have, seen what I wasn't supposed to see. Clearly I was never to mention any of this again. My confusion turned to anger. I was angry at the suffering I saw. I was angry that God's love seemed so impotent. I was angry that

I couldn't speak my mind and get some answers. I was angry that the church I had put so much hope in turned out to be so deaf, dumb, and blind.

Then the anger turned to fear. *What if God found out what I was thinking? What if God knew that I was secretly raging inside?*

I discovered there is a vault inside of us waiting to secure those kinds of secrets. When something has hurt or frightened us, we can drag it down the treacherous steps to the dark dungeon below and leave it there for safe keeping. Then we go about our business as if it's not even there. I locked my disappointment, confusion, and anger at God in that vault and promised myself I would never think those thoughts or feel those feelings again.

Through it all, however, one thing hadn't changed: I still needed God. I needed someone to pray to. I needed to believe there was someone out there who might take an interest in me if I behaved well enough. I needed God, but I didn't trust Him. There was just too much evidence of abandonment—a growing list of stories proving, more often than not, that God turned His back on those who suffered.

It was a very twisted combination of feelings—needing so desperately the source of my rage. So I did the only thing I could think of—I learned to pretend.

I pretended in church on Sunday mornings. I would bow my head and mouth the prayers. I pretended I could live without the answers to certain questions. I pretended I had no secret. I pretended to believe what I was supposed to believe. I looked the other way when God's love fell short. I practiced my religion in much the same way the child of an alcoholic parent creates a whole mythology of excuses in order to live with the anger, loneliness, and desperation that comes from the abandonment: "Daddy's just sleepy tonight." "Momma didn't mean to say those things, she's not herself." For me it was, "God works in mysterious ways."

The great theologian Frederick Buechner reminds us, "We don't just have secrets; we become our secrets." Whatever has been locked in the vault—abuse, trauma, abandonment, betrayal, the suicide of a parent, anger at God—these secrets are never silenced. We may think they are confined to the dungeon below, but in truth they are active participants in our lives calling in plays from the sidelines, appearing anonymously in our decisions and relationships, wearing any number of baffling disguises. Finally our secrets, unbeknownst to us, become the unauthorized biographers of our lives, exerting such a death-grip that finally we are little more than actors mouthing the scripts that are shouted at us relentlessly from someplace deep within.

* * * * * * * * *

Twenty-five years after first questioning if "Jesus Loves Me," I sat in the chapel with the freshman class of Drew Theological Seminary. The dean, robed in academic splendor, greeted us with these troubling words: "You have all entered the ministry for the wrong reasons. Many of you will never graduate. As for those of you who do, I hope it is for the right reasons."

I looked around the chapel at the other new students and wondered what reasons they had for entering the ministry. As for me, I was there to face my secret, once and for all. I found out very quickly it was far more difficult than I imagined.

In our world some secrets can be spoken. If we have been physically, sexually, or emotionally abused, there are places we can go. Highly trained professionals are available to help us. Groups of similarly wounded seekers are ready to welcome us, embrace us, make us part of the family. Likewise, with addictions, compulsions, and other habits that ravage our lives, if we have the guts to admit it, if we are willing to tell someone, help is on the way. We'll be praised for our courage; we'll make new friends; we'll feel as though we've finally come home.

But there is one unspeakable secret. If trauma and suffering have built an impenetrable wall between us and God, if we have searched our soul and still can't stomach the idea that a "God of love" seems so content to turn His back on those in need, if we are devastated by the loneliness and desperation that come with feeling this kind of abandonment; if this is our secret, then we are alone. There is no place to go. No one will listen.

If this is our secret, we are the problem, not the victim. Those in the helping professions tell us to "get on with your life, grow up." Religious professionals, after a few understanding nods, will ultimately dismiss our feelings as just another sin in need of forgiveness. Instead of finding help, we will run up against a conspiracy of silence. If we tell someone how we feel, we won't be seen as courageous but as dangerous. When anger at God is the secret, it is still acceptable practice to blame the victim. This anger is the most terrifying of all emotions and the most sacred of all taboos. To break the silence is to turn the world upside down.

If the committees of lay people and clergy who presided over my candidacy process had known my motivation for entering the ministry, they never would have allowed me to do so. I was there because every other attempt had failed. I was there because I believed that, through the ministry, I could gain access to the secret vaults of the people I served. I didn't want access in order to exploit anyone or to hurt anyone. I wanted to see if anyone shared my rage.

Four years later I graduated from Drew Theological Seminary and was appointed to my first church. Then something happened I hadn't planned on—I fell in love with my work and the people I served.

Despite the fact that the profession has been maligned of late, being a minister is still an amazing experience. Even with the mountains of administrivia—fund raising, building maintenance, budgeting—I found countless opportunities to share in people's joy at Sunday picnics, graduations, baptisms, weddings, camping trips with the youth, long conversations with the elderly on lazy, hot afternoons.

I experienced abundant kindness. My parishioners have been enormously patient and encouraging, especially in the early days when I felt terribly awkward at most ministerial tasks—especially preaching, which used to make me shake with fear.

In time, I discovered other unexpected blessings. Once I earned my parishioners' trust, they granted me the sacred privilege of walking with them through some of life's most difficult moments.

When we sit with people by their death beds; when we help negotiate a truce to their domestic violence at 2:00 a.m.; when we listen to the grisly details of rape, incest, abuse, or other violence they have suffered; when we pray with them over a dying child in the intensive care ward; when we bury their loved ones, we hear things others don't hear.

When we carefully opened the vault, parishioners old and young—bankers, potash miners, school teachers, housewives—spewed forth floods of rage born of a grief that never goes away. There is a silent, suppressed rage in our world, born of a grief that never goes away.

I discovered a strange irony in the tears I cried on that Mexican beach. For years, my parishioners confessed their anger to me so I could help them heal. I found countless others who shared my secret; I was no longer alone. I was the one they came to with their anger. I was the one they trusted. I was their hope for healing, but they never knew I had nothing to offer, nothing to say.

They bared their souls to me, told me things they may never have told another human being and I sent them away empty-handed. As their minister, I should have been able to ease their pain. How could I, when I never opened the vault of my own secret? In response to their pleas for help, I unconsciously repeated the same maddening words I'd been running from all my life: "God works in mysterious ways."

* * * * * * * * *

As I headed home from Mexico still haunted by my secret, I planned to avoid it again by busying myself with ministerial duties. I might have succeeded in keeping my secret memory safe forever if it weren't for a tragic phone call and a young girl named Cheryl.

CHAPTER 3

Forbidden Fruit

> Of all the trees in the garden
> you may eat, sayeth the Lord.
> But of the tree of the knowledge
> of good and evil, you are not to
> eat, for on that day you eat of it,
> you will surely die.
>
> —*Genesis 2:17 KJV*

Only a few days after Christmas, decorations on local storefronts were already in various stages of undoing—a dismantling process not at all unlike a circus packing up its big top and leaving town. The aerosol snowmen stenciled onto the windows at Burger King were pockmarked from the wind and scarred by children's curious fingernails. The plastic Santa at Jiffy Lube had lost an arm. What was supposed to be a star above Kmart had so many burned out lights it now looked like a giant "Connect-the-Dots." Ironically the only fully intact decoration I saw as I drove that night was the lurid blinking message above one of El Paso's strip joints: "Piece on Earth."

Finding the address among El Paso's dizzying labyrinth of suburban sprawl was, in itself, an experience of grace. Finally there it was—the dream house the mother had told me about.

"You'll have to come see us real soon," she had said. Neither one of us anticipated it would be this soon.

The dream house had only one dim, yellow light burning on the porch. Fortunately the door opened before I had to try and locate the bell.

"I'm Julie. I'm a neighbor," said the woman in the doorway. "Please come in."

"Where are the children?" I asked.

"Across the street with my husband," she whispered.

"And where's..."

Before I could finish my question, she pointed silently down the long, dark hallway where I could barely make out the silhouette of a woman sitting on the edge of the couch. She was curled in a fetal position, her hands clutching her knees.

The thick, new carpet fought back as I walked. As I got a little closer, I began to recognize her features.

She was a plain woman in her mid-thirties, quite frail. Smudged mascara streaked down her cheeks making her look almost as if she'd been physically beaten. From an artificial Christmas tree across the room, ghostly red, green and blue shadows danced across her dress.

How odd, I thought, to see her sitting alone in her dream house wearing the same blank expression so many homeless people have when the only thing they're sure of is that they have no place to go.

"Janey?"

She raised her head, stood up, stumbled over to me and put her arms around my neck. I had to hold her up because she barely had enough strength to stand. It was a little awkward for both of us. We hardly knew each other and now I could feel her hot breath on my neck and her damp face against my cheek.

"I needed someone to be here with me when I told the children," she gasped.

I just held on to her. I didn't know what to say.

With a nod, Janey sent her neighbor to get the children, and slumped back onto the couch. I sat beside her, holding her hand. Her five-year-old son entered first. Without saying a word, he headed right to the TV and turned on his Nintendo. When his sister arrived, she stood frozen in the doorway with a look of sheer terror on her face.

Janey reached her arms out in silence. When the daughter still wouldn't budge, she said, "Honey, please, come sit down."

Children know. The young girl looked around the room and saw her mother crumbling beneath the weight of some mysterious, unbearable pain. She had only two words to say, "Where's Daddy?"

"Cheryl, please sit down."

Shaking, the girl darted her eyes around the room. "Something's happened to Daddy. He's been hurt. Tell me where he is! I want to see him right now!"

With the last few drops of strength left in her, Janey began talking very slowly, "Cheryl honey, Daddy's been in an accident."

Cheryl's lips quivered. "He's gonna be all right, isn't he? I want to go to the hospital to see him. Momma, can we go right now?"

Janey approached her daughter and reached toward her face with a trembling hand. "Honey, Daddy's been in a very bad accident. Cheryl," she looked longingly into the child's eyes, "Daddy's dead."

Cheryl burst into a tortured, agonizing dance. Flailing her arms in all directions, she clenched her fists and punched wildly—first into the air, then into the couch. Her mother, the neighbor, and I watched in an almost reverent silence as Cheryl leaped from the couch and raced around the room. While she ran, she screamed at the top of her lungs the bloodcurdling cry of a mortally wounded animal.

She began hitting herself, mostly in the face. When we yelled at her to stop, she ripped at her clothing and tore her hair. The mother tried to approach, but Cheryl's look warned her to stay away until the dance was over.

I felt a strange distance, as if I were watching a movie. As she swirled and yelled in pain, I sat frozen. The whole scene became a blur. When it finally came back into focus, a different movie was playing.

A few weeks earlier, Cheryl, looking so pretty and innocent, stood before the congregation with a group of other children and their parents. It was Confirmation Day. Amid boys squeezed into jackets and ties, and girls wearing frills and curls and their first make-up, Cheryl stood out.

While the others looked around self-consciously and appeared more than a little bit bored, Cheryl seemed deeply moved to make a public commitment to her faith.

"Do you here, in the presence of God, and of the congregation, renew the solemn promise and vow that was made in your name at your baptism?"

"I do."

"Do you confess Jesus Christ as your Lord and Savior and pledge your allegiance to His Kingdom?"

"I do."

"Do you receive and profess the Christian faith as contained in the scriptures of the Old and New Testaments?"

"I do."

"Do you promise according to the grace given you to live a Christian life and always remain a faithful member of Christ's holy Church?"

"I do."

The sharp crash of breaking glass brought me back. Cheryl had taken a lamp off the end table, yanked it from the socket, and thrown it against the wall. The mother, fearing further injury, ran toward the young girl and wrestled her to the ground. I never moved.

I thought of Helen Keller as I watched the two of them, their arms stiffened at the elbows reaching clumsily for each other, as if blinded by their shared heartbreak. Four hands touching, grasping, searching each other for something that was lost. A mother stroking the wet cheeks of her daughter. A child clawing helplessly at the one who brought her into this world.

Janey, now as hysterical as her daughter, cried out to her, "Oh, baby, baby, baby." Cheryl responded with a string of obscenities she was too young to know.

I don't know exactly how long it went on, but, finally exhausted, Cheryl collapsed into her mother's arms gasping for breath. A few moments later, with the tree lights still blinking and the electronic racket of Nintendo warfare rattling in the background, Cheryl began a prayer of sorts, composed of the most frightening words I had ever heard. In a sore-throat whisper, she repeated: "I hate you, God. I hate you. I hate you."

Julie, the neighbor, glared at me. "What are you doing here?" she demanded, as if I were some intruder caught snooping around the house.

Unlike me, the neighbor did something of real value that day. She took the kids into her home, fed them junk food and showed them videos while Janey dealt with the police and the medical examiner. Upon Janey's request she'd called me because Janey thought a minister—someone who'd seen tragedy and human suffering many times before—would know what to do and say. He could find the right words. He'd do the right thing.

Ignoring the neighbor's curt question, Janey reached out a forgiving hand and invited me to join Cheryl and her. As I moved closer to them, honest words struggled to emerge, not from my gut, but from the part of me that remembered being a child making his Confirmation. Instead, they were stifled by familiar—no, *involuntary*—phrases wanting to spill from my lips. "God works in mysterious ways," I might say, or "Jesus loves you."

I was now the Confirmation boy in my new suit with the too-tight collar. The altar I was approaching was two broken-hearted people huddled together for dear life.

But before I could mouth the words, Cheryl raised her head from her mother's breast with a look that left me speechless.

In part, it was the "I hate you, God" anger still burning in her eyes—the blood thirsty rage that comes from being an innocent victim caught in the jaws of tragedy, discovering that despite your best behavior and all your solemn Confirmation promises, God refuses to lift a finger to help.

As I looked deeply into her reddened eyes, I saw a strange helplessness far more disturbing than her anger. It brought back memories of a thousand other heartaches and crying voices.

I recalled sitting in the living room with a young woman who had just lost both her children on Mother's Day. I remembered waiting in the intensive care unit with two young parents while their little boy struggled for breath after being hit by a car. I remembered the gurgling coughs made by a friend's child who suffered from cystic fibrosis—a sound that always made me want to puke with sorrow. I remembered the tears of the potash miner when he showed me the scars where his father had hit him with a whisky bottle, when he was just a boy. I remembered a hero I once knew who couldn't dress himself anymore so he sat on the edge of the bed staring at his feet not understanding what was wrong—six socks on one foot, none on the other. Alzheimer's is what the doctors called it. "Hell" was the word my mother used.

As Cheryl stared with those strange, helpless eyes, my involuntary phrases choked me. Till then, I had always been pretty good in these kinds of situations. Nodding my head, lowering my eyebrows, a strategically placed, "Uh-huh" or "Umm, I understand," I wore the face of professional concern well.

I felt her anguish, too. Beneath the professional veneer my heart would break. I guess that's what most people have chosen to see in me and why over the years I've been entrusted so many times with the secrets of people's deepest pain.

I've learned that when trauma strikes, in whatever form—death, illness, heartbreak, addiction—our carefully built structures of meaning and hope can crumble to the ground. That's why the experience of being invited into someone's trauma has the same eerie feeling of what it must be like to search for survivors following an earthquake.

I think, If I get there in time I can follow the cries, try to lift the rubble, bandage the wounds, and hold the injured as tight as I can in an effort to stop the bleeding. In the moment, I talk to the victim, assure him I'll be there, not just for the moment, but for the long haul. Surrounded by debris, I discuss rebuilding and remind him that his future still awaits. But while helping him find even a small measure of mercy among the smoking wreckage, I secretly hope that the conversation never includes the question "Why? Why did this happen to me? I've tried my best to do what is right; is this what I deserve? If God is love, why does He let this happen? Why!" I carefully guard against letting the conversation get out of control.

Despite my best intentions to help, that awful question always puts me on the defensive. It reminds me of the unfairness of life, an issue which causes even the most articulate philosophical or theological system to stutter. More than just breaking the rules, asking "Why?" is, in effect, a kind of treason because this is the question we have all agreed to forget.

If these questions persist it's just a matter of time before the words of sympathy lavished on the victim will take on a different tone: "Don't be foolish. You're acting like a child. Snap out of it."

Of the many taboos passed down from generation to generation, the one that transcends cultures, races, and religions is an ancient covenant: When life holds a knife to your throat, your cries of pain, as loud and persistent as they may be, must never amount to anything more revealing than name, rank, and serial number.

We ask "Why?" at our own peril. There is little tolerance for those who break the code of silence.

With fervent prayers we cross-stitch fragments of hope together into a homey quilt suitable for framing—even if only part of a single, frail wall is still standing and a single crooked nail is available. They read, "God Is Love," "He never gives you more than you can handle," "The Lord is my Shepherd." By avoiding "Why?" we can replace the damaged structures of meaning and hope brick by brick and our cross-stitch platitudes can distract us from the flaws that lie behind them.

This is how I have seen tragedy play itself out in the past. I would get the phone call, rush to the home or to the hospital, listen, do my best to let them know I cared, and then when it was time for me to leave, we would say a prayer together that went something like this: "Dear Lord, thank you for your blessings. We know you have a special purpose even in this sorrow. Help us believe in you. Amen." One last embrace and then we parted.

If anger at God was an issue, I steadfastly refused to listen. I would head home convinced that the code of silence had been maintained, the taboo unbroken. That's the way it always went. But not tonight.

Cheryl had found the place where angels fear to tread. She would not be comforted. She would not play by the rules. She would not be silenced. She would not plea-bargain her misery, her pain, or her hatred of God. She wanted the world to know she was innocent and, given a fair hearing, she would be vindicated by a jury of her peers.

Just then, I finally understood that the strange helplessness I saw in her eyes was not hers; it was mine. It is one thing for her to feel abandoned by the faith she professed. It is quite another to be a representative of that faith.

Something snapped in me. I wanted to scream so badly because now this whole frightful night was not just about Cheryl; it was about every hurt and heartache, every tragedy I had ever seen. Worse still, it was about my hurts, too. I wanted to tell Cheryl it was all right to be angry. I wanted to tell her she should feel that way, that she should shake her fist at heaven and curse God from the bottom of her soul.

I wanted to tell Cheryl that underneath my Confirmation suit was a person just like her. I wanted to scream with her then for all the times I myself should have screamed but didn't. I wanted the neighbor to hear my screams. I wanted the church to hear my screams. I wanted God Almighty to hear my screams, to see who I really was and to know how I really felt. Even in my deepest moments of sorrow or pain I have always managed to smother my screams of anger with prayers of fear and obedience: "Dear God, just give me the strength to get through this. I know you must have a reason." That's what I prayed. But it wasn't what I felt.

Cheryl whispered once again those frightening, unspeakable words: "I hate you, God. I hate you. I hate you."

She had nothing to be afraid of, nothing to lose, no reason to hide what she felt. I knew at that moment, if she had the chance, she would have plunged a knife into God's heart and danced in His blood.

* * * * * * * * * *

The Biblical story says that waiting somewhere near the center of each of our lives is a tree that offers the knowledge of good and evil. Mostly we live our lives, you and I, as best we can trying to love, to forgive, to find some grace and peace, trying our best to avoid that tree.

Yet, one day, through no fault of our own, the world crashes in on us. In the end, it is not so much that we look for the tree, but rather, the tree finds us when we are most vulnerable.

One lonely, wintry El Paso night it happened again. Like a story from long ago:

"Of all the trees in the Garden, you may eat,"

sayeth the Lord. "But of the tree of the

knowledge of Good and Evil, you are not to eat,

for on that day you eat of it, you will surely die."

But the serpent said to the woman: "No!

You will not die! God knows that on the

day you eat it your eyes will be opened

and you will be like gods, knowing good and evil."

There on the floor sat a young girl, the bittersweet juice of forbidden fruit dripping from her chin. Her saddened expression wasn't burdened by fear, remorse, or shameful nakedness. It merely said, "Go and banish us from your sight again, God. Lock the gate on whatever remains of Eden. At least this time we'll know we deserved it."

When the young girl had eaten her fill, she offered the fruit to me.

CHAPTER 4

On the Tip of the Tongue

To me there's more things broken,

Than anyone could ever see.

Why the angels turn their back on some,

It's such a mystery to me.

—*Bonnie Raitt*

The funeral was on Thursday. Janey, numbed with Valium for the occasion, managed all the obligatory motions with robotic precision. Her little boy huddled next to her on the church pew, shiny new loafers dangling high off the floor, his head buried in her lap.

Cheryl had aged over the last few days. Her once warm hazel eyes had lost their sparkle. The softness had drained from her face. Her fragile innocence now shattered, she reminded me of one of the teenage runaways who drift like tumbleweed along Sunset Boulevard. She spoke to no one.

Several friends of the family stood up to say kind words about the deceased. As I sat waiting my turn, I stared out at the crowd: two hundred people stuffed into the small chapel fidgeting nervously on the hard benches. Some held handkerchiefs to their faces. The air was thick with the sour smell of hothouse flowers and formaldehyde.

For some reason I found myself thinking of a woman who had taken care of our children many years ago. Nellie was a round, red-faced woman who had been through almost as many husbands as she had waitressing jobs. Now in the autumn of her life, she had settled down anonymously in southern New Mexico in a little, still-life cowboy town where time had ground to a halt some forty years earlier. I loved Nellie and her kindness and patience toward my children. I especially loved her broad, toothless grin and her jelly-belly laugh. She said it was good to laugh every day even when there was nothing to laugh about. "Laugh at life as much as you can," she always said. That's why I was so surprised one day to see her crying.

She and I sat at the parsonage's rickety dining table. As awkward strains from my son's piano lesson ground in the from the other room, Nellie began a story. She started quietly, but continued in earnest. The story may have come from a real experience or from the vivid imagination of a young girl. Either way, it tapped a mythic revisionist interpretation of my own past hurts and expressed a truth that has stayed with me ever since.

Nellie's father was a lumberjack. She and her mother, along with three brothers and five sisters, grew up in a southern logging town.

Late one afternoon her father was deep in the woods working feverishly to make his quota before dark. The first early winter snowfall was filling the skies and blurring his vision.

When the shark-toothed saw blade finally finished ripping through the huge tree trunk, her father wiped his brow with an old handkerchief and cried out, "Timber!"

He stood back and listened for the hush that fills the air when a tree falls—that moment of silence the forest observes when it loses one of its own. Safely out of harm's way, the lumberjack watched the old tree land softly on the snowy ground with hardly a whisper. As darkness blanketed the hillside, he called it a day.

Only when he turned to leave did he feel the sharp pain. With cold horror he saw what he had done. Despite his best efforts to keep things under control, he had cut too far through the trunk and sliced a deep gash into his own leg. When he didn't return that evening, a search party went after him. They found him in knee-deep snow, lying in a frozen puddle of blood. Nellie hadn't been allowed to join the search. Instead, she waited at home taking care of the younger children. It was midnight before the men carried her father into the house. He lived only long enough to tell the story.

Silence in the church snapped me back to the present. It was my turn to speak. Putting the ministerial polish on the funeral required looking past Cheryl's ravaged glare from the front pew. It demanded that I dull the impact of her hellish dance the other night and hush the voices that, since then, repeated her vicious prayer, "I hate you, God. I hate you." I had to smother my own rage at God and share a message of faith and reassurance even though the taste of forbidden fruit still burned on my tongue. I had to do what ministers are supposed to do. Or so I thought.

As the congregation waited for the minister to speak, I found myself as far from him as they. With them, I watched him walk slowly to the podium, his long white robe flowing behind him. He had developed a strategy over the years which helped him minimize his nervousness in front of crowds. If he unfocused his eyes just slightly, then the faces would begin to melt together and the room would become a soft, manageable blur.

Likewise his facial muscles were as dependable as a spit-polished regiment of Marines. The routine was automatic: frown slightly, tighten the lips, pause thoughtfully, lift the eyebrows, let the shoulders rise with a full breath, then ease the air out with a slow and meaningful sigh. Bring the right hand to the chin, then higher to allow for an unnecessary adjustment of the eyeglasses. Straighten the notes on the podium.

"Let us pray," he said. Two hundred heads fell forward.

"Almighty God, who art leading us through the changes of time to the rest and blessedness of eternity, be thou near to comfort and uphold. Make us to know and feel that thy children are precious in thy sight, that they live evermore with thee, and that thy mercy endureth forever. Thankful for the life which thou has given us for these seasons, we pray thy help now to resign it obediently unto thee. Assist us to return to the scenes of our daily life, to obey thy will with patience, and to bear our trials with fortitude and hope. Amen."

The minister talked about hope, heaven, and helping each other get through the pain. Some students from the high school where the deceased had taught stood before the gathering and offered a squeaky, sobbing "Amazing Grace." Then the minister gave the benediction, followed the casket down the aisle to the back of the church, and waited to greet people on their way out the door.

"Lovely service, Reverend," they said politely. Some of them, speechless with grief, rushed past without a word and went straight to their cars.

After everyone was gone, the funeral director smiled and put a check in my hand. I took off my robe and packed up my notes. When I turned to leave, the sharp pain hit. Grief and sadness overwhelmed me. The pretense, the make-believe, the looking the other way; the defense of God Almighty that I took upon myself Sunday after Sunday piously telling people to blame themselves for any suffering they experienced, to look to their own hearts for sin, to stop deceiving themselves and just come to the altar and confess, surrender, and then feel the healing power of God's love—it was all choking me to death.

In a darkened, deserted parking lot, alone in my car without any fanfare or a single witness, the house of cards I had built my life on came tumbling down. The faith I had been raised on, the faith I promised to uphold and represent, all of it was gone. The words I finally spoke—first in a whisper then screaming at the top of my lungs—came far more easily than I ever imagined, as if they had always been there on the tip of my tongue.

CHAPTER 5

A Preexisting Condition

All the lonely people,

Where do they all come from?

All the lonely people,

Where do they all belong?

—Lennon and McCartney

In the mid 1970s, the movie *Network* introduced us to a man named Howard Beale and his unforgettable experience with rage. Beale is a hard-nosed, no-nonsense journalist who clawed his way to the top of his profession. Now in his late fifties and anchoring a national news broadcast, he has money, fame, fancy parties, and high living. But something about Howard Beale isn't quite right.

The symptoms come on slowly. The drinking, he reasons, is part of the cost of doing business and a proper reward for a hard day's work. His relationships with coworkers are cold at best, but what could one expect under the pressure of ratings? Mostly he is so absorbed playing the game that he doesn't give any of these things a second thought.

One day his world falls apart. Like a jigsaw puzzle crashing to the floor, Howard Beale hits bottom and the pieces of his life scatter in all directions. Suddenly nothing fits. Everything is disconnected. Nothing makes sense. After all those years of painstakingly assembling his career, Beale is now in the middle of a jagged-edged, odd-shaped picture he no longer understands. He feels alone. Isolated.

Beale doesn't start out full of rage. That comes later. First he feels a pervasive, gnawing sadness, an emptiness, a brokenness, a kind of homelessness that follows him around each day like a ball and chain. A few people try to help, but no one likes these symptoms in themselves or others. Fearing they'll catch whatever he has, those around him pull even further away.

He tries to deny his problems. Soon, however, the symptoms become obvious even to Beale. Then the worst happens—his audience recognizes the change in him and his ratings plummet.

He isn't all that surprised when the boss calls him into the office: "It's only business, Howard. I'm sure you understand. We'll have to take you off the air."

Beale has a big problem. Not only does he feel like a stranger in his own world, but he also senses a danger he can't quite name. He's running for his life but has no idea what's chasing him.

This dilemma creates a terrible tension in the film. Why is he feeling this way? If Howard Beale's symptoms followed in the wake of some awful event, his behavior would be perfectly understandable and we would call his condition—with its desperation, despair, anguish and hopelessness—*grief.*

But this once very successful man hasn't suffered any great trauma or loss. No biopsy comes back malignant; flood waters don't reduce his home to rubble; no lunatic murders his wife and children.

Network is the story about *another* kind of grief—a grief we all share. It lives beneath the surface of our lives as an underlying current of "dis-ease." We know it by a number of familiar names—despair, brokenness, separation, loneliness, depression, anxiety, fear. Like an old, unhealed wound, this other grief is the preexisting condition we bring into any traumatic experience.

Like Howard Beale, many of us appear to manage this condition fairly well by pursuing things like success, love, religion, risk, and comfort, and by leading a life that has as many distractions as humanly possible. Keeping a safe distance from this wound is critical to our sense of personal safety, security, and happiness.

When trauma crashes into our lives, shock, pain, and suffering don't shatter our world. In these frightful moments, the old unhealed wound rises to the surface, meets us face to face, and laughs a hideous, mocking laugh at our straw fortresses and the hocus-pocus promises and prayers we were counting on to help us steer clear of any suffering in life.

The reemergence of this wound generates tremendous self-doubt. We already have a proven record of failure when it comes to resolving grief. If this wound is still with us despite a lifetime of efforts, why should we believe we'll be any more successful dealing with the trauma at hand? When we secretly whisper to ourselves, *I may never get over this*, it's not simply the voice of shock or self-pity; it's probably the truth.

The idea that we have a preexisting condition, another grief at work in each of us long before any traumatic event comes into our life, is a very ancient notion. Since ancient times, we've been aware of this preexisting condition. We know this other grief simmers in each of us before any traumatic event invades our life. Only recently have we expended such effort to avoid acknowledging and discussing it.

Consequently, we're often left wondering, "What is the nature of this wound?" "Where does it come from?" "Why do we have it?" "Does everyone have it?" "How does it affect our lives and our relationships?"

Scores of explanations, theories, philosophies, sacred stories, and myths try to identify the source of this preexisting condition. Generally speaking, these explanations seem to fall into three broad categories. Each carries with it important influences on how we understand ourselves, our relationships, and the way we live our lives.

Guilt: A Theology of Grief

One of the most familiar and influential stories of the origin of this preexisting condition appears in the book of Genesis. After Adam and Eve eat the forbidden fruit, their brief sense of exhilaration quickly gives way to a number of troubling side effects—they feel frightened, lost, vulnerable, and separated. Naked and ashamed, they are strangers in paradise, hiding in the bushes and expecting the worst.

Their disobedience changes not only *them*, but we are told that it also changed the world and all generations to follow. No longer welcome in the Garden of Eden, Adam and Eve are thrown unprepared into a dangerous and painful world where they are at odds with themselves and with each other and destined to search their whole lives for what they have lost.

According to Genesis, our preexisting condition is a self-inflicted wound. These feelings of homelessness, brokenness, and separation, says Genesis, are received at birth as an *inherited* wound. Throughout our lives we continually reinjure this wound through disobedience. We are the source of our own suffering.

Many people point to the book of Genesis as one of the origins of the Just World theory—the belief that God is good, righteous, and perfect and all problems in life, whether physical or relational, are directly the result of our disobedience. Indeed, much of the Old Testament is a series of human dramas in which this belief is played out repeatedly in the lives of individuals and communities: If you're good, then you are rewarded; if you're bad, you are punished. If a child is born dead, the parents have sinned. If an army captures your city, you must have displeased the Almighty.

Why has the theology of guilt endured throughout the ages?

In part it's because the equation seems fair: You do the crime; you do the time. But there's another reason for guilt's longevity. Basically, the alternative is just too frightening: If human disobedience hasn't created such a dangerous world, then what has? What kind of Creator would make a world with so much suffering?

For a good part of the 20th Century, guilt had a stubborn public relations problem. It was seen by many as an unenlightened vestige of the past, an outdated impediment to good mental health. However, during the last decade we have been revisiting questions of personal responsibility, and some of the constructive power of guilt is once again beginning to surface. In truth, when it comes to guilt, it's not the poison, it's the dose. As motivator or deterrent, guilt can sometimes bring the best out of us. Guilt can remind us of our commitments and promises. It can keep us from acting on every lust. Guilt can make us try just a little bit harder even when we don't feel like it.

Is guilt the cause of Howard Beale's problems? Is he hiding some terrible transgression in the bushes? Should he seek forgiveness, make amends?

Beale does spend some quiet moments combing through his past but quickly concludes that his sins are nothing out of the ordinary and couldn't possibly be the source of such a difficult predicament. He isn't perfect, but who is? Others are far more corrupt and brutal. Why is he the one dangling from a thread? There must be some other reason, but what could it be?

He gets more and more desperate. Showing a deadly flair for the dramatic, Beale tells the audience that for his *grande finale*, he will blow his brains out on national TV. Burning with whiskey and desperation, he looks at the camera, puts a gun to his head, and starts to squeeze the trigger.

It seems for a moment that the conclusion is written in stone, that nothing can stop him. Is this dramatic self-destruction inevitable? Is it his destiny?

Fatalism: A Philosophy of Grief

Like the idea of a Just World, the philosophy known as fatalism also appears to have developed near the dawning of civilization. In contrast to the theology of guilt, fatalism locates the source of the problem outside of the individual.

Fatalism teaches that there is an immutable preset pattern to life. The events and circumstances we experience are determined by some distant, unknowable, uncaring, and often nasty force greater than ourselves. We have very little to say about how our lives unfold.

Some extreme forms of fatalism can be hazardous to our health. The Kamikaze pilots of World War II, like their modern pop culture counterparts—Kurt Cobain, Jim Morrison, Jimi Hendrix, Janis Joplin, who set their lives on a collision course with our cherished sensibilities and then dutifully self-destructed—are some of the more grisly, lethal examples of the effect fatalism can have on the human spirit.

Nonetheless, fatalism has been an attractive philosophy throughout history primarily because it appears to take us off the hook. If the source of our preexisting condition is beyond our control, then there is no reason to feel guilty or responsible for our behavior. For those seeking a license for sex, drugs, and rock 'n roll, or those just weary and frustrated from trying to make sense of human suffering, fatalism has always been there with open arms ready to accept our resignation.

If fatalism were truly the guiding force behind Howard Beale, however, he certainly would have pulled the trigger. Instead, something inside of him *clicks*—probably his survival instinct. What the audience witnesses instead of a dramatic suicide is a dramatic transformation. Suddenly Howard Beale is furious.

Beale puts the gun down and begins a long speech starting with these now famous words: "I'm mad as hell, and I'm not going to take it anymore."

It is a thundering homily about the craziness of life; how we don't fit into this world; and no matter how hard we try, things don't get better. On and on he goes, getting madder by the minute.

The producer in the control room starts to pull the plug on the broadcast, but then he looks around and sees everyone transfixed by what Beale is saying. Pacing like a caged animal, frothing at the mouth, Beale pushes the limits: "All of you out there in TV land, tomorrow night I want you to join in with me. When I give the word, open the window of your home, stick your head out and scream at the top of your lungs, 'I'm as mad as hell and I'm not going to take it anymore.'"

Exhausted, he walks off stage.

Is he a madman? Will the audience play along? Does anyone share his rage?

Evolutionary Psychology: The Genetics of Grief

The idea of a preexisting grief has received growing attention lately because of the work being done by a relatively new science called evolutionary psychology. Some of the more notable leaders in this field are Randolph Neese, Robert Wright, and the husband and wife team, John Tooby and Leda Cosmides.

Basically this theory is an expanded version of Darwinian natural selection, the belief that human characteristics were developed or eliminated because of their ability to contribute to survival. For example, rising from all fours allowed our ancestors to use their hands for other purposes, while walking. Likewise, our bodies were molded and shaped in many other ways to provide advantages in battle, childbirth, food gathering, etc.

Evolutionary psychology takes Darwin's theory one important step further by claiming that natural selection shaped not only the human body but also the human mind—especially the emotions. According to this theory, the mind is like any other organ, bone, or muscle of the body; its mission is to aid in survival. Therefore, our mental impulses and emotions—lust, warmth, joy, humor, fear, anger, etc.,—were kept, shaped, or discarded according to their ability to contribute to survival. For example, feelings of romance, passion, and lust are valuable because they can motivate us to seek out a mate. Warmth and joy might have remained with us because these emotions can help bind a tribe together and create a higher level of safety.

Unlike a theology of guilt or philosophy of fatalism, evolutionary psychology sees our preexisting condition as a natural consequence of our relationship to our environment. Despite evolution's best efforts, there can never be enough adaptations made on our behalf to even the playing field adequately. We are at a permanent, insurmountable disadvantage, genetically mismatched to the threats we face. At birth, Mother Nature whispers to each of us, "Checkmate." From that moment on, our best maneuvers, strategies, and delaying tactics can only prolong the inevitable. We are players in a game we can never win, given a grief we can never resolve.

Is Howard Beale hearing the echoes of "Checkmate" ringing in his ears?

At first glance these explanations of our preexisting condition seem very different and, presumably, any thoughtful person would surely choose one over the other. However, these theories are probably better understood as being somewhat interdependent and, rather than choosing one over the other, we tend to invite some combination of the three into our lives. We can probably remember moments when we have seen the world through each of these sets of eyes.

Most critical, however, is understanding that these theories have a common message: Resolving grief is always a larger issue than dealing with any particular trauma because *trauma is not the root cause of grief*. Trauma is salt on an old wound.

If we were able to unravel all the mysteries of what happens to a person during trauma, and we wove that information into a flawless grieving process that left no stone unturned, then we worked that process to perfection, giving it all the time, care, and nourishment it required. If we were surrounded the whole time by the unconditional love of family and friends, then the very best we could hope for—if we were 100 percent successful—is that maybe we would be able to remove most of the salt from the wound.

Once trauma re-opens the wound, it tends to remain near the surface—more painful and raw than ever. Sometime later we begin to experience what are probably the most troubling long-term effects of trauma. The career, material comforts, and especially religious beliefs and practice—those things we could previously counted on to successfully keep the wound at bay—no longer provide the same results after trauma. Consequently, we never get back to "normalcy" again.

Mad As Hell

Network's climactic scene is riveting because it's hauntingly familiar.

When Howard Beale challenges his viewers to join with him in his rage the following night, no one knows what will happen. After all, isn't he just a madman?

The production crew gathered in the studio for the show are so quiet they can hear the heartbeat of the person beside them. When Howard goes on the air, everyone holds his breath. Without a moment's hesitation he tells his audience, "Go to your windows right now, stick your head out the window and scream at the top of your lungs, 'I'm as mad as hell, and I'm not going to take it anymore!'"

People join in. Men, women, and children, in the streets of the cities and the countryside, feeling their fears suspended for a few sacred moments, scream at the top of their lungs what has long been their most carefully guarded secret. A tidal wave that may have been forming at sea since the beginning of time finally crashes on the shore and floods the earth with rage.

* * * * * * * * * *

Each visit with my father was more crushing, more disabling than the last. If there are demons in this world, surely Alzheimer's disease is one of them. It has no conscience, no mercy, and it isn't satisfied until it has stripped every last shred of dignity from the victim and torn the hearts from the caregivers.

The wound that I first experienced as a child—the brokenness, separation from God and anger, the senseless suffering of the innocent—I had kept pretty much at bay with education, friends, family, religion, and the seven-day-a-week commitments of professional ministry. But the trauma of watching someone I loved disintegrate before my eyes had forced the wound to the surface.

I felt betrayed by my faith. The only God I knew was a God I could no longer trust. Angry, lost, and desperate, I began searching for something to believe in; something that would give my life meaning and purpose; something that could heal the wound, understand the depth of my grief; something that would give me the life-changing, earthshaking experience I needed.

My search for peace and healing brought me through many spiritual, philosophical, New Age, and self-help strategies. I practiced meditation. I prayed. I sat on a psychiatrist's couch, met my inner child. I went through success conditioning believing if I only tried harder, if I were more disciplined, if I learned to work the process, then the wound would heal and the promised acceptance and new life beyond my grief would greet me with open arms.

* * * * * * * * * *

If you have read this much of my story, then chances are it is in some way your story, too. Trauma, like a ravenous pit bull, has sunk its glistening teeth into your throat and no matter how much time passes, no matter how much effort you expend, despite the love of those around you, it just won't let go.

You once believed that this was a Just World ruled by a loving God who cared about His children and that if you played by the rules, you could count on some fairness, mercy, and maybe even a little protection. That belief helped you feel safe and gave meaning and purpose to your life. Now all of that has been shattered.

You have listened to the advice of caregivers and followed dutifully the grieving process giving it all the time, patience, and courage you could muster. But instead of leading you to acceptance and a new life, you feel more like a dog chasing its tail round and round in deepening circles of despair.

At times you are overcome with rage, wanting to shake your fist at heaven and scream bloody murder at the God who watched you suffer and never once lifted a finger to help. But scared to death at what might happen if you did, you bury that anger deep inside and remain silent, taking it out instead on yourself or those around you. Perhaps, like me, you finally came to the end of your rope. You may be there right now.

One otherwise ordinary day, the shocking, earthshaking miracle, the only thing that could ever have saved me from my grief and anger crashed unexpected into my life. When all hope was gone, when I was dangling helplessly by a thread, something happened that changed me forever.

The pages ahead are the road I took to that miracle.

| CHAPTER 6 | *America's Self-Helpnotic Trance* |

> I had to admit that even after
> years of recovery and working on
> myself I still felt a baffling despair
> about love and fulfillment.
>
> —*John Bradshaw*

Bookstores are filled with promises. The colorful, artsy covers reaching out from the shelves offer us just about anything we can imagine: travel to exotic places, stories of romance and courage, business tips, biography, history, even glimpses into the future. None of the promises are louder, more insistent, or as seductive, however, as those found in the self-help section, where titles seem to scream like concessionaires on the Atlantic City boardwalk: "Be thinner in five days." "Seven secrets to better sex." "CHANGE YOUR LIFE!" You can have it all—health, wealth, love, and happiness—we promise.

Over the last 25 years or so the publishing industry has exploded with a tidal wave of self-help books, each offering game plans that are supposed to transform us into better people. These promises have sold millions of books.

Because we Americans love to reinvent ourselves, we find these promises irresistible. They feed a burning hope. If we put our noses to the grindstone, then we can overcome anything that bothers us—hurts of the past, addictions, grief, low self-esteem—and become the sexy, wildly successful, powerful, possibility-persons we were meant to be. We want to believe there's a new world waiting for us someplace out there, and if we can just find the right Moses with the right list of commandments, we can walk tall and proud into the Promised Land and live happily ever after.

But I wonder: are we thinner, saner? Do we have stronger families, better children? Are we more sober? Has this billion-dollar industry produced real, measurable results?

This year many more of us will wander down the self-help aisles. Like children in the grocery store lusting after the trinkets in cereal boxes, we'll reach out for more sugar-coated promises. Will these promises change our lives?

Self-help is nothing new in America. It came over on the Mayflower and has been with us in one form or another ever since. But some of the lessons that once made self-help an effective vehicle for lasting change in people's lives have been long forgotten.

The New World Order

Early adventurers to the New World were chasing glowing promises of a "shining city on the hill" and a "New Jerusalem." The messages they heard from the pulpits, on ghetto street corners, and down the dark, dank walls of the debtor prisons, were positively explosive: "There is a New World waiting, a chance to begin your life again. You don't need to be victims of circumstance anymore! In the New World, *anything* is possible."

Like the rivers and forests, rich soils and minerals, the inner landscape of the human being seemed another frontier to be conquered, its natural resources similarly exploited to produce individual wealth, success, and power.

Personal transformation had a specific inner architecture and strategy comprised of three essential components:

- **Teamwork.** Personal transformation is not a solitary task. It takes teamwork. Enthusiasm, commitment, and discipline are effective only when they are used within a community of people who are trying to accomplish the same goal. *"You can't do it alone."*

- **Standards and expectations.** Community requires mutual responsibility, accountability, social, and even economic interdependence and an acceptable code of behavior that is clear to everyone and expected of everyone.

- **Spiritual foundation.** Personal transformation is a spiritual task. Change of identity is the result of a change of heart, *conversion*, getting right with God. This new healed relationship with God is the fountain from which the new identity and changed behavior flow, day by day.

Modern self-help strategies are still pretty good at remembering the importance of community, accountability, standards, and expectations in creating personal transformation. In the area of spirituality, however, one of the most basic ingredients necessary in making it all work seems to have been long forgotten.

Whatever Happened to Religious Freedom?

The search for religious freedom was a driving force that brought many of the early settlers to this country. They were looking for a place to worship as they pleased and practice a spirituality of their own choosing.

The Old World's unholy alliance of church and state taught our early settlers some important lessons about religious freedom. They understood that religious oppression wore two very different faces: restriction and neglect. Many of us are familiar with the restrictive form of oppression. If we force everyone into one religious point of view with narrow, prescribed forms of worship and expression, we cut off creativity, subvert spiritual growth, and generate lots of anger and frustration.

Our ancestors knew that religious neglect can also be a form of oppression. An environment that leaves people to fend for themselves, outside any system at all, without any spiritual guidance can be every bit as damaging as forcing them to accept a specific form of religious expression. Without structure, there can be no religious freedom.

To our modern minds, this formula for religious freedom seems like a contradiction in terms. "Doesn't freedom
of religion mean freedom from structure? Isn't structure
what they were trying to escape? What about individuality?"

The Myth of the Noble Spiritual Savage

"Let me find God my own way, on my own terms. I
don't need you to tell me how to pray, how to worship, or
what to believe. I can do it better all by myself." This is one
of the most costly misunderstandings of spirituality in our
modern world, and it is at the very heart of the self-help
movement.

If people are just left alone to explore their own longings, we are told, unencumbered by any kind of religious
structure, they will be able to reach out to God and build a
lasting, meaningful relationship. Like Rousseau's "noble
savage" who is naturally in tune with Mother Nature, the
self-help movement has a mythological image of the "noble
spiritual savage" who, when left to his or her own devices,
will naturally be at one with God. It's a nice ideal, but does
it work?

I saw the results of this kind of thinking very early in
my career as a minister when parents in the community
brought their children to the church for baptism. Many of
these young couples had received no spiritual training
whatsoever. Their parents, in turn, had been careful not to
force them into any specific kind of religious structure.
What they envisioned, I suppose, was a freedom of choice

---

that would allow their children to become spiritual butterflies going from flower to flower gathering spiritual nectar along the way.

What happened instead was something quite different. When left to peruse their own spirituality without any guidance and structure, people ended up confused, exhausted, and empty-handed.

A World of Road-Less Travelers?

John Bradshaw's PBS television program first introduced me to the world of self-help. Bradshaw tried to reach beyond psychological behaviorism into the world of personal mythology and encouraged his audience to revisit and heal the hurts of the past by embracing what he called the "inner child." Bradshaw, also an Episcopal priest, clearly emphasized spirituality as a critical to the success of his system—a spirituality of one's own choosing.

I believe it was in a dentist's office that I first came across a book called *The Road Less Traveled*, written by Dr. Scott Peck. For years this book could be found most anywhere, from the Sunday school classroom to hospital waiting rooms, even in the corporate boardroom. Peck maintained that when it came to spirituality, the destination mattered less than the willingness to sample a broad variety of ideas and experiences along the way. To a generation raised on suffocating theological absolutes, this blatant permission to experiment was a positively explosive idea.

As for the most difficult questions about human suffering, Peck responded, "Life is a mystery" and suffering is just part of the game. To weather the storm, we need spirituality—of our own choosing.

I went on to read many self-help classics, including those by Norman Vincent Peale and Og Mandino. Both authors preached the power of positive thinking and the necessity to reach' out to God in my own way, if I wanted lasting personal transformation.

Although I recall very few of their titles, each book memorably took great pains to suggest that personal transformation requires spirituality. According to these books, in order to accomplish anything—weight loss, sobriety, grief resolution, better relationships—"We must have the help of a Higher Power." Conspicuously absent from these discussions, however, was any concrete guidance on how to find this Higher Power.

"It's all a mystery; you're on your own." "Just leave me alone and I'll make my own peace with God." It sounds liberating...until the loneliness sets in.

Sadly, those who follow this advice usually discover that lack of spiritual guidance is not freedom at all, but a pernicious form of spiritual neglect. Our modern ignorance about the real meaning of religious freedom has given birth in America to a whole generation of road-less travelers.

The Hard Work of Religious Freedom

Our natural instinct to explore and experience the sacred never imbued us with a natural ability to find it on our own. Spirituality is learned behavior; we learn by doing.

Fundamentally, spirituality is a form of communication, a language. Just as we would never send a person off by herself into the woods to learn how to speak, neither should we expect someone to develop a meaningful spirituality on her own.

In virtually every culture around the world, those wanting to experience the sacred seek the counsel of others who have been there before them. The seeker is then carefully guided through the teachings, traditions, and rituals of a structured system. To abandon someone in his search for the sacred, to leave him to his own devices rather than take him by the hand along a well-trodden path, would not be considered freedom at all, but the worst form of spiritual neglect.

That's why we need a starting point, some basic guidance. We should be allowed to invent a new religion if we want to, but we shouldn't have to.

How then, if structure is so important to a meaningful spirituality, does individuality find expression?

Where Does Individuality Come From?

Have you ever gone through the rigors of learning to play a musical instrument or watched someone else try to do it? Learning to play music and finding a meaningful spirituality have some important similarities.

Each begins with a longing. Before we ever pick up an instrument and try to make our own music, we have already discovered that the world is filled with sounds, rhythms, and musical patterns: the tapping of the woodpecker, the beeping of car horns in traffic, the rustle of autumn leaves, the whistle of a teakettle. Some of us find these sounds so captivating that we want to make some of our own.

It's incredibly exciting to hold the instrument in our hands until the initial shocker hits: "How in the world am I ever going to make music on this thing?"

Disappointment can set in after just a few music lessons. Music is not the free-for-all it appears to be from a distance. Those beautiful sounds are not left to chance; they are the product of structure and discipline.

The energy, enthusiasm, and wonder that bring us to music must be focused in such a way that certain ground rules can be learned: octaves, harmonies, scales. Music has definite boundaries. There are, for example, places on the instrument where we cannot successfully produce a note. If we go outside the boundaries, all we get is noise or silence.

If a child comes to us and asks for the opportunity to learn a musical instrument, should we tell her, "Go and learn it by yourself"? Fearing that her freedom of expression might be compromised by any kind of structure, do we make her invent her own musical scale? Trying to protect her artistic individuality, should we refuse to nourish her in the tradition and compositions of the great masters of the past?

If a budding musician ever demonstrates any real individuality, it will be because he first learned the importance of structure. Individuality is always a derivative function of structure. Musical creativity doesn't happen by accident; it is dependent upon a deep knowledge of structure and tradition. We get that knowledge through commitment, guidance, and practice. The same is true of spirituality.

Like the love of music, spirituality also begins with a great longing. I believe that we sense from our earliest childhood years that there's a God out there someplace and we want and need a relationship with that God. The *why* of spirituality is self-evident, even instinctive. The real question throughout the ages has always been *how.*

We're busy working for a living, paying the mortgage, raising the children, trying to remember to put the garbage out on the curb on Thursday evening. With all the headaches and challenges of life spinning around us in a million directions at once, is the best advice we can expect from our spiritual leaders the suggestion to "go do it yourself"?

The myth of the noble spiritual savage who can naturally find God on his own has been a very costly misunderstanding. Even the greatest spiritual masters that history has ever produced—the prophets, sages, saints, and saviors—all carefully trained in the spiritual traditions of their cultures from teachings deeply rooted in spiritual structures. None of them reinvented the wheel. The revelations they offered us were simply new ways of looking at old truths. Ignoring the spiritual lessons and traditions that have gone before us is not only foolish, but it's also the height of arrogance.

Another misconception often expressed by those fearing any structure in spirituality is that it produces a uniform, religious experience—a mindless army of programmed automatons who nod and pray the way they are told. Nothing could be further from the truth. In fact, there is no such thing as a uniform religious experience.

I have always felt that one of the highest honors of ministry is the opportunity to serve communion. In that very holy moment each person receives the same bread, the same wine; nonetheless, the experience of communion is as different as the people who participate.

This ritual has the power to generate endless varieties of emotions and images within individuals. Some feel joyous; others are lost in their tears. For some, it is a very private moment. Others want to reach out to everyone around them. The ritual of communion is a meticulously structured vehicle for individuality. Spiritual structure, like the bars and key signatures of a musical scale of good musical structure, doesn't inhibit creativity, it releases it.

A God of My Own Choosing?

The self-help industry has been very careful to make a clear connection between grief and the need for spirituality. Most any book on the subject of grief will insist that spirituality is necessary for long-term success and recovery. The weight of grief is too heavy and the road is too long to try and go it alone. We get shipwrecked too easily during the day; grief is bigger than we are. With that in mind we're told to go into our heart and get in touch with our Higher Power—the God of our own choosing we're told to "Reach out to God, *as we understand Him*."

This advice, as gentle and caring as it may seem on the surface, is not as innocent and benign as it pretends to be.

If those of us who are grieving had an understanding of God that was healthy, effective, meaningful, healing, and accessible; if we had that kind of help at our disposal, then wouldn't we already have put it to use? Would we really need a self-help book to tell us to go and do it?

For most of us, a God of our own choosing might very well be the *last* respite for healing. Wasn't it the God of our own choosing who was nowhere in sight when trauma ripped our heart into a million pieces? Wasn't this the God who ignored our suffering and was silent when we cried out for help? Trusting in a God of our own choosing would likely be a death sentence for recovery.

The why of spirituality is self-evident. The real question is how. How do we find a God that not only answers the "why?" of grief but also the "how?" of relating personally to Him? Can we find the guidance and structure we need? Is there even a God out there we can trust?

CHAPTER 7

Virtual
Spirituality

We miss something, Mercury.
We miss the poignancy of the transient,
That sweet sadness of grasping
For something we can never hold.

—*Zeus to Mercury*

Someone turned off a switch and blackness covered the city. A hush went over the tens of thousands who had gathered at the stadium. Even the TV commentators were speechless.

A single lighted match pierced the night and revealed a solitary figure standing high on a platform. He wore the garments of a mythical figure from long ago, a garland of flowers around his head, and a crossbow strapped across his back. He slowly placed the match at the tip of an arrow and it burst into flames. Carefully, methodically, he fitted the stem of the fiery arrow into his bow and slowly pulled back the string.

You may have forgotten all the other details of the 1992 Summer Olympics in Barcelona, but you probably will never forget how they began. The archer attempted to shoot a flaming arrow hundreds of feet through the night air and light the Olympic torch. He had only one chance to accomplish this feat in front of a worldwide audience of more than a billion people.

The camera centered on his steely face. His eyes were more than confident, they were defiant. The muscles in his arm pulled back the string, tighter and tighter. For just a moment he froze like a Greek statue. Then, with the world holding its breath, he sprang the catch and sent his arrow streaking like a comet across the night sky.

Far more rode on that arrow than just the expertise of a marksman, the dollars of TV ratings, or even the reputation of the Olympics. Riding on that arrow were the dreams of every person who wants to believe that anything is possible.

Somewhere near the time of the Barcelona Olympics, I found myself back in the bookstores looking for hope. Disappointed by the empty promises and vague spirituality of self-help literature, I was now open to just about anything. Wandering up and down the aisles, I found myself in the New Age section.

New Age spirituality claims that anything is possible. It promises soaring flights to the stars, strategies for controlling every event and circumstance of life, finding one's dream lover, dancing with the angels, talking with the dead, and finally, the ultimate accomplishment, assuming one's rightful place as a god. I was about to embark on a fascinating journey.

My experience with New Age literature began with a book by Dan Millman titled, *Way of the Peaceful Warrior.* To this day it remains for me a very magical book.

Millman is a great storyteller with disarmingly simple style. Before I knew it, his dialogue and descriptions pulled me inescapably into the story. *Peaceful Warrior* is Millman's autobiography, the story of how he met his "Higher Power," in the form of a wise old gas station attendant who guides him through the inner universe in search of peace and fulfillment.

Beyond being a great story, Millman's book is something of an anthology of New Age philosophy. Skillfully woven into this dramatic story line are many of the roots of New Age: Eastern religions, New Thought, Scientology, Science of Mind, and a good dose of magic. *Peaceful Warrior* is an example of New Age spirituality at its very best—playful, fun, outrageous, stubbornly optimistic, and more than a little tongue-in-cheek.

New Age literature has made some important contributions to the modern spiritual quest. First, it reclaims much of the playful nature of spirituality, which has somehow slipped through the fingers of mainline religions whose rituals, sermons, and worship can be dry and lifeless. The New Age reminds us that one of our greatest gifts as people is our imagination. Spirituality should be fun.

New Age teachings are also an important step beyond most other self-help literature because the movement understands that people need more than just permission to be spiritual, they need guidance and structure. New Age teachings go beyond vague generalities and offer specific step-by-step strategies for spiritual connection.

Most important of all, however, New Age directly addresses a critical part of the emotional and spiritual brokenness which is so pervasive in our culture. Many people have faithfully followed the teachings of the churches only to have the "give your heart to God and He will take care of you" theology fall short when they needed it most. They have found that surrendering one's life to God and receiving forgiveness of sins don't always prove to be the life-changing events they were promised to be.

On the surface, it may just seem like disinterest or boredom, but those who have reached out to the church only to walk away empty-handed often live the rest of their lives with a great deal of frustration, cynicism, and anger: "If what the church is selling truly reconciled me to God, then why wasn't God there when I needed Him?"

Understanding that so many people are unfulfilled by organized religion and often angry with the church for championing a God who can't seem to be trusted, the New Age makes this tantalizing promise: Through meditation and the power of the mind, we take back control of our lives. We can determine, in advance, the events and circumstances we desire. We will no longer be dependent upon the whims and fancies of an unpredictable God. We can channel the energies of the universe and become one with God. Given enough time and effort, we can perfect the ability to shoot a flaming arrow through the darkest night of any hurt, problem, or limitation. We are limitless. Nothing is impossible.

Creating Our Own Reality

The single central premise of New Age belief is that every event in life can be traced back to a thought. Nothing happens by chance. There are no accidents. Everything happens for a purpose as the direct result of the power of our minds. Through a mental process called "manifesting," we create our own reality. As Sanaya Roman, channeler for a spiritual being called "Orin," puts it:

> Your thoughts have real substance, although your scientific instruments can't yet measure them. You might imagine your thoughts as magnets. These magnets go out into the world and attract the substances that match them; they duplicate themselves in form. Everything around you was a thought in someone's mind before it existed in your reality …you are an unlimited being, you can create whatever you want. (p. 32)

This process, also known as "magnetizing" what we want, is central to most New Age books whether the general topic is channeling, crystals, or witchcraft. Therefore, much of the information in these books details various meditation exercises and techniques designed to help us focus our thoughts, decide what we want, and then take appropriate mental actions. If we take the time to get in touch with our higher self, we are told, our deepest desires will be revealed to us along with the best strategies for rapid success. In this way we "create our own reality."

The most far-reaching version of "magnetizing" and mind control I ever personally encountered was a process called Time Line Therapy. This technique promises the ability to focus the power of the mind so directly and precisely that we not only create the events and circumstances we want in life, we actually predict their exact moment of occurrence. Here's how it works:

> Relax, take a deep breath. Feel the friendly spirits all around you. Let your heart lead you far off into space. Rise way above the earth. Dance among the stars. Be playful. You are light, you are weightless, you are eternal. You are divine. Greet your Higher Self. He will counsel you on what lies ahead and how you can control every aspect of daily living.

Looking down from high in outer space, we use our imagination to picture a highway stretching out beneath us. Somewhere near the center (depending on our age) is a circle which designates our present position in life. The highway goes in two directions: back toward the past and forward into the future. Like planning a vacation trip, we alone will decide what we will experience along the way.

This process not only predicts the future, it also claims to heal the past. The first task is to travel back along our Time Line to visit certain key moments of our past. Only after clearing negative emotions can we make sure our future will be as bright as we want. It may take conventional therapies months, even years, to help us make peace with the past, but Time Line Therapy claims to do this in about an hour.

Let's say there was a particularly painful moment in childhood that still haunted me. The instructor would have me go past the event to an earlier time and then look forward on the time line toward the future, pretending the event is no longer there. Poof—it's gone. Or is it?

Once I heal my past, I can plan the rest of my life. I achieve any future plan by picturing in detail what I want and placing it within a kind of frame, like a painting. Then I place the framed picture along the future time line at the precise date of my choosing.

I took this course in Time Line Therapy with a group of about 25 others. After four weeks we each had a notebook full of dreams reaching toward the future from three months all the way to the next 30 years. I did as instructed, planning out all the details I wanted—my career, friends, travel, future home, material items—until I was about 70 years old. I stopped planning at that point, thinking I should leave a little room for spontaneity. Exactly as instructed, I placed each of these desires along my future time line and expected to watch in blithe amazement as one prediction after another materialized.

Blaming the Victim

After a few weeks my carefully planned future began to unravel. I had paid my money and followed directions, but something must have gone wrong. When I contacted my instructor and asked him why none of my predictions was coming true, his answer revealed the flaw of this kind of "virtual spirituality." My instructor blamed me for his system's failure. I hadn't tried hard enough. I didn't work the process. I messed up on the fundamentals. Worse still, I didn't *trust*.

When New Age doesn't work, it blames the victim. Any shortcomings are attributed to the individual. Because the system is a divine channel, the inevitable source of any problem with it must be the channeler. The failure, then, is not the responsibility of some higher being, it's because of us. We are to blame.

For all the fine-tuned hype heralding the New Age as a creative, modern alternative to stuffy, organized religion, a closer look reveals it has some striking similarities to, of all things, some of the more radical versions of fundamentalist Christianity.

- **Channeled scriptures.** Both can believe their sacred writings have been "dictated" from a Higher Source. Both offer a progressive connection with the divine based on personal achievement and initiative: The better we are, the closer to God we get. We must do the right things, learn the right prayers or meditations, memorize the scriptures.

- **Control the future.** Both are often used as attempts to control the future. While New Agers use a crystal ball or meditation to create their reality, fundamental Christians use obedience, prayers and financial support as leverage in bargaining for comfort, protection, and success.

- **Blame the victim.** When the system fails, blame the victim. When I asked my Time Line instructor why the system didn't work, his reaction reminded me of the way revival faith-healing preachers scream at people in wheelchairs who don't have enough faith to "get up and walk!"

Finally, although both approaches are marketed to the consumer as populist alternatives to the perceived emptiness of organized religion, in the end they can create within the individual the very same sense of betrayal, anger, and cynicism they condemn in other systems.

The dream of controlling all aspects of life is an ancient human longing. "If only we were gods," wouldn't the possibilities be intoxicating? Just think of it, a virtual reality life where we put on an electronic helmet and gloves and experience only what we want—no more traffic jams, no sickness, no more crabby bosses to deal with; all the people around us obliged to act according to the scripts we write for them. We could have whatever we wanted, whenever we wanted it. Paradise, right?

Although the initial possibilities of such power seem inviting, controlling everything would unbearably complicate and burden our lives. At what point would we create our own realities, or predict and schedule all of life's events? When we are children? Would we create our future based on the perceptions of a ten- or twelve-year-old? Or would we wait until college when we're balancing our need for freedom with a nagging identity crisis and pressures from family to "get a life"?

When planning the events of our future, would we have the foresight to include things like disappointments, heartache, deadlines we couldn't meet, even failure? If we created a life without these kinds of challenges, how would we ever develop the higher human qualities of courage, patience, hope, and forgiveness? If everything went exactly the way we wanted, *what kind of people would we become?*

Fortunately, all the systems for controlling the events and circumstances of life share one important quality: They are all doomed to failure. The fabric of life always includes a randomness that even the clearest crystal ball or our best behavior, prayers, and discipline can't control. Even if we could muster enough effort, money, and luck to control 95 percent of what happens to us, the 5 percent that alluded us would have a greater impact than the 95 percent we were able to control.

New Age followers claim that their system reconnects us to God, but does it ever reveal an understanding about why we feel disconnected? Do New Age enthusiasts know what really hurts? Why are they so silent about our anger and frustration at God? Do they really think that, after years of brokenness and spiritual homelessness, we can simply meditate our way back to God? Truth is, we can't do that any more than we could jump across the Grand Canyon; the gulf is just too wide and dangerous. No amount of crystal-gazing will cure it. We can't achieve our way to God either. There isn't enough success in the world to completely, permanently numb the pain.

The Basics of Healthy Spirituality

Spirituality can work only when we fully understand what makes it work. Throughout history, whenever spirituality offers people a genuine, long-term connection with God and produces inner changes that impact life, it successfully addresses two basic issues:

- The limits of human nature

- The meaning of human suffering

Embracing Our Limitations

We are not magicians or gods expected to eliminate the chaos and randomness of life. Rather, we are like sculptors facing the unpredictability, the mistakes, mishaps, and broken promises—all the imperfect, raw material of each day—as if it were an unpolished, jagged piece of stone. Our task is to fashion it into a thing of beauty. Spirituality, when it works, is an art form, an act of creativity.

But how do we sculpt spiritual beauty? Contrary to New Age teaching, the first critical step in creating a healthy spirituality is being willing to accept our limited nature as human beings. Psychiatrist Rollo May reminds us that our limited nature, far from being our enemy, actually plays an extremely important, positive role in our lives.

Human consciousness is born out of the awareness of limits. The infant makes a critical discovery the moment he understands that the shiny, red ball in the crib is not him. The ball begins where his body ends. As May writes in *A Cry for Myth*, "Through a multitude of limiting experiences we learn to develop the capacity to differentiate ourselves from other objects" (p. 56).

Ironically, confronting our limitations expands our experience. In much the same way as musical structure gives birth to individuality, limitations give birth to creativity.

Higher Consciousness

The sonnet, elevated to celestial heights by William Shakespeare, is an exacting form of poetry with a rigorous structure of 14 lines. Conforming one's passion, vision, pain, and ecstasy into such a demanding framework is a formidable task for the poet. Unlike free verse, where the poet operates without the constraints of meter or rhyme, the sonnet is a beautiful demonstration of how embracing limitation and form can be vastly empowering. Sonnets can live forever. Says May:

> The very necessity of fitting your meaning into a form requires you to search in your imagination for new meanings. You reject certain ways of saying it, you select others, always trying to form the poem again. In your forming, you arrive at new and more profound meanings than you had even dreamed of. Form is not a mere lopping off of meaning that you didn't have room to put into your poem; it is an aid to finding new meaning, a stimulus to condensing your meaning, to simplifying and purifying it and to discovering on a more

universal dimension the essence you wish to express (p. 16).

The empowering quality of limitation and form is illustrated in a measurable way during Olympic competition. Athletes aspiring to set a new world's record work for most of their lives trying to slice a mere fraction from the current record. To be successful the contender needs a variety of good information: high-tech training techniques, the proper form, nutrition, etc. But the single most important piece of information the athlete can have is something much more basic: The athlete must know what the current boundaries are. The limit drives the athlete. The runner must know what he's chasing. If the poll vaulter had no cross bar, how high do you think he would jump?

The awards ceremony at the Olympic games is a moment of great splendor and pride. There are roses, national anthems, and tears in the eyes of winners, losers, and spectators. At that moment the gold medallist is considered to be the best in the world. He or she might have even set a world's record. By setting a new standard, cutting a fraction off the old record, or raising the bar another inch, the athlete has created a new form, a new boundary, and, ironically, another limitation.

Similar to athletics, any artistic endeavor must begin with an understanding of the boundaries—the size and shape of the canvas or stone. Without limits there can be no art because, as May explains, true creativity comes not from ignoring boundaries, but from the passionate tension of struggling with them. In the end, the boundaries expand just a bit. This is the authentic, creative act.

Spirituality is another act of creativity that must begin with boundaries and limits. Formless and unstructured it becomes destructive. We need to know where the boundaries begin. Even in the womb, if a baby were to kick and stretch without ever finding boundaries, it would experience a terror beyond description. We carry the need for boundaries within us our entire lives.

We are not gods and no amount of meditation is going to change that. We are limited creatures. As Dante reminded us many years ago, "We are half angel and half animal." The so-called "higher consciousness" described by the New Age—zooming through the galaxies, melting blissfully into the vast limitless and formless universe—has been attractive bait for a generation of baby boomers. Unfortunately, higher consciousness is something entirely different than what the New Age has in mind.

True creativity is not the discarding of form, but as Rollo May reminds us, "the progressive revealing of new forms." The authentic artist takes the hazardous journey into higher consciousness and returns with new forms.

The central idea of New Age literature—that human beings are limitless creatures—is a recurring theme in history. It is also, perhaps, the most damaging untruth of all time. As brutal as some religions can be in their demands—nit-picking prescriptions for behavior, intolerance of free-thinking—the tragic lie that we are by nature limitless creatures is far more destructive. The fragile wings of this kind of belief always melt and the once soaring believers fall, like Icarus, into an even deeper ocean of despair.

But what about the archer at the Barcelona Olympics? When the arrow landed dead center and the torch exploded in flames, didn't the archer prove to the entire world that anything is possible?

No. But he shaped the boundaries of his own abilities into a magnificent work of art. Through his stellar achievement, he challenged us to raise our expectations for the beauty of the art we could create.

A powerful truth was on display that night, but not what first met the eye. The arrow could be only so big. The torch could be only so far away. The archer did something much more important for us than try to prove that we are limitless.

Frustrated with unsuccessful attempts to control our lives, we are now beginning to accept, once again, our limitations. Indeed, our current fascination with angels reflects, in part, our struggle with our limitations.

In a poignant, childlike way, the world has fallen in love with angels. Jews, atheists, conservative Baptists, and channelers all seem to appreciate them equally. As a result, angels have established some common ground among usually contentious religious groups. In angels, these groups have something to talk about, something to share.

It's a step in the right direction because deep down it's a cry for help. We are realizing that life is just too tough, we can't make it on our own. In our moments of desperation, we hope an angel will come and make a difference in our lives.

But believing in angels, in itself, is not sufficient spirituality. Angels, it turns out, have their own limitations. Even the smartest angel can't answer our toughest question: "What is the meaning of suffering?"

Making Sense Out of Human Suffering

Ultimately, what we seek from any spiritual system is not wealth, power, or the ability to control life. All of that, even if it could be achieved spiritually, would have very little meaning if we couldn't make sense of the suffering in life. "Why do people suffer if God loves us so much?" is the question that launches (and ends) most spiritual journeys.

The New Age may be silent about our anger and frustration at God, but it has much to say about human suffering. In 1965, two Columbia psychology professors claimed to have been "scribes" for the series of writings now known as *A Course In Miracles*. The book was authored, they claim, by Jesus Christ.

The *Course* is described as having "one function and one goal": to offer us "the choice to heal the deep inner illness that is the source of our pain." The *Course* teaches that we are ruled by a "mind-set of extreme separateness and attack, a condition of mental isolation in which we look upon the world through condemning eyes of judgment and anger." This mentality throws us into a "state of war with ourselves, crippling us with the guilt and walling us off in icy loneliness out of fear of the world around us."

So far it sounds pretty good, but the explanation offered by such New Age proponents is rather astonishing. *It is all an illusion*, says the *Course*—the separation, loneliness, fear, broken relationships—an illusion.

The answer? "Choose, instead, to see the light of Heaven in everyone and everything we look upon, reaching out to the world in a new relationship, one based on love, joining, and giving."

The *Course* claims to be a wake-up call. We are all asleep, and we can accomplish much of this New World simply by waking up. Through a number of exercises the *Course* teaches how to perceive the world in a new way. Then we become "innocent, peaceful, and joyously happy."

But what about the source of our misperception—the anger, frustration, sense of abandonment, the wound? It would be wonderful if we could simply wish all this pain away, but if we could, wouldn't we all have already done so? Yes, we all want to see the world and each other differently, but changing perception is far more involved than simply waking up.

Nonetheless, people love to hear this message. *A Course In Miracles* has sold millions of copies. *Course* teachers like Jerry Jampolski and Marianne Williamson have spoken to packed houses all over the country. Ms. Williamson was often interviewed following the September 11, 2001, terrorist attack. When asked if we should feel angry at God, she quickly dismissed the question saying it was not God's fault, and we should look inside ourselves for greater strength. Reporters should have asked her what she believed about human suffering.

The *Course* teaches that suffering is an illusion. We don't really suffer, we don't really have pain; these are incorrect perceptions. If we would just wake up, it would all go away. This suggestion implies a depth of heartless cruelty beyond description.

I have held dying AIDS patients in my arms. I have performed burial services for children and suicide victims. I have seen Alzheimer's, drugs, rape, and family violence ravage people's lives. I know for certain suffering is *very* real. I can't think of a more destructive thing to tell a grieving person than her pain is an illusion. If you don't believe me, ask a New York City firefighter.

Human suffering is the source of our deepest separation from God. Unless our spirituality is somehow able to deal with this issue, it is worthless.

CHAPTER 8   *Our Deepest Fear*

> We now feel we can cure the patient without his fully understanding what made him sick. We are no longer so interested in peeling the onion as in changing it.
>
> —*Dr. Franz Alexander*

Chairs in the aisles, herds of cars spilling out of parking lots and into the street, standing room only, half-read newspapers left abandoned on kitchen tables, TVs silenced for the first time in five days, suits and ties, dresses and heels—on Sunday morning September 16, 2001, America went to church.

It has been estimated that 84 percent of Americans went to houses of worship on the weekend following Ground Zero—throngs of frightened seekers, trying to pray, looking for hope, doing their best to find comfort in God. In an event later described as "seismic" by Martin

Marty, a professor emeritus at the University of Chicago and a religion scholar, Americans went looking for God.

As the weeks went by, did the throngs remain? Were the parking lots still full? Did people find what they were looking for? When we see our carefully built structures of meaning and hope crumble to the ground in the wake of trauma, does our collective search for God make it a "seismic" spiritual event? Or does it become seismic only because, despite our best efforts to find God, so many of us again give up the search empty-handed?

Grief is spiritual, *deeply* spiritual. In time, the wreckage of trauma can be carted away, the smoke will clear, and even the visible structures can be rebuilt. The event that once brought us so much pain mercifully starts to fade into the past and, even to those who know us well, it can look pretty much as though we have gotten on with our lives again. But under the surface lingers a deep sense of betrayal, a nagging fear that we are no longer safe, a perilous separation from a God we thought we could count on to protect us, and a growing anger oozing from our decision to accept blame for suffering we didn't deserve.

After trauma breaks our hearts and changes our lives, one thing remains the same: We will still be spiritual persons. We will still have a hunger for God. The wound will still haunt us with questions about our purpose in life, the meaning of suffering. We will wonder if there is an afterlife, and grapple with a host of other innate longings that follow us all the days of our lives. We'll never stop looking for something that can heal the brokenness and give us peace.

Through love and acceptance, we'll try even harder to bridge the dangerous, impossible gulf between us and our Creator. We will need to believe in something that brings us hope and gives meaning to our everyday lives, even though the answers we once trusted in have scattered—just dust in the wind.

Can we ever find faith again?

Centuries of spiritual searching are behind us. The world has had prophets, saints, martyrs, theologians, many varieties of Holy Scriptures, and thousands of books to explain their messages. We can turn on the TV any time and find televangelists, or reruns of *Providence, Touched By An Angel,* or *Davy and Goliath* each offering its own take on the meaning of life. On Sunday mornings, churches everywhere invite us to try their brand of salvation. Despite all this support and guidance to choose from, spirituality remains one of the most difficult concepts to understand.

Why is spirituality so treacherous? Why do even our best efforts inconsistent, incomplete, temporary results? Why does spirituality seem to fail us when we need it most? What's wrong?

What Is Spirituality?

A little girl kneels by her bed and says the Lord's Prayer; an old rabbi runs his gnarled fingers along familiar cracks in the Wailing Wall. Is that spirituality?

Is spirituality found in a teenage boy's efforts to memorize portions of the Koran? Should we look for it in the face of a political prisoner on a hunger strike, a nun bathing the sores of a leper, a philanthropist giving her riches away to the poor? Is spirituality something we can see?

Not necessarily.

A person could kneel at a church altar to receive the Sacraments and all the while be thinking of having an affair. Someone else might bow his head to pray and find himself plotting to destroy his enemy. Acts of kindness and compassion can be self-serving; forgiveness is sometimes used as a weapon. All kinds of crazy things are done in the name of God.

Spirituality is not so predictable. It seems as likely to strike like lightning into the heart of an unsuspecting atheist as it is to arrive as the result of a carefully planned regimen of discipline and self-sacrifice on the part of the most enthusiastic believer. (Mother Theresa's personal journals describe long bouts with spiritual emptiness and feelings of separation from God.)

Spirituality is deeper than what we can see, deeper even than what we believe.

Spirituality Is Instinctive

I once had a grammar-school principal tell me that parents, whether they want to or not, are always teaching their children. For parents, teaching is not optional; it's part of everyday life. The real focus should be on the children. While their teaching is a given, the lessons they're learning are optional.

Spirituality operates in our lives in a similar way. Spirituality is not optional. We're not invited to be spiritual; we're drafted for life. This reality has nothing to do with whether we ever set foot in church, read the Bible, the Koran, or Confucius; or whether we ever learn to meditate or pray.

We can try not to be spiritual, but we will fail. We can swear off all the superstitious, narrow-minded fundamentalist or knee-jerk liberal teachings we were force-fed as children; we can convince ourselves that we're atheists. We can discard all religious teachings; all concepts of God; all understandings of the church, heaven and hell, the Ten Commandments, Buddha, meditation, yoga, and the New Age, but we won't be any less spiritual when we're through. In fact, our spiritual journey may just gain a whole new lease on life—still looking for the same answers although this time in different places.

Even if we give up and resign ourselves to the likelihood that we may never find a spiritual home, the frustration, heartache, confusion, and anger we feel every time we think of spirituality is, in itself, just another spiritual path. Unbelievers, heretics, brokenhearted blasphemers, cultured despisers of religion we may be; nonetheless, the journey goes on weaving itself through our everyday lives with or without our permission regardless of whether we consciously participate. Only the results are optional.

We can't give up. We can't stop. We can't throw in the towel because spirituality is not fluff, luxury, obligation, or wishful thinking. *Spirituality is survival.*

The Roots of Spirituality

If we don't know it before then, we all learn about survival instinct in high school biology. When we feel threatened, our bodies produces an adrenaline rush that tightens our muscles, focuses our thinking, puts us in a heightened state of alertness, and prepares us to take some kind of action.

Then our brain offers us a choice: Stay and fight the enemy or turn and run as fast as we can until we are safely out of danger. This neurological mechanism known as fight or flight happens within us without our permission or participation. Although we credit our survival instinct for keeping us out of trouble, we seldom acknowledge that this fight or flight instinct is limited and fraught with all kinds of difficulties.

Fight or flight can only help so much during a plane crash, terrorist bombing, gang rape, or incest molestation. Indeed, sometimes our survival instinct can actually become toxic. For example, if I had a daughter wasting away from anorexia or a son addicted to crack, this enormous threat isn't my war to win. Nonetheless, my survival instinct would still faithfully pump me full of adrenaline as I do my level best to remain calm.

Fight or flight does not determine survival. Our survival instinct does not have a crystal ball; it can't look ahead and see which choice would be more effective. The real key to survival is *diagnosis*, a clear understanding of the nature of the threat. Only then can we take appropriate action. Our survival instinct can help us become aware of danger; it can prepare us for action. If fight or flight could save us in every jam, we might not need spirituality.

But the survival instinct has limitations. We're not perfectly adapted to all environments. In the face of most threats, we seldom feel safe and powerful and competent, even with adrenaline rushing. We don't always have the tools to protect ourselves at the moment we need them. By recognizing the limits of fight or flight, we can appreciate the need for spirituality. It does all the survival instinct cannot.

Surviving the Wound

The survival instinct must see our preexisting condition as life's most menacing threat. The condition leaves us no place to run or hide. It also reveals our permanent wound. Most painfully of all, under the wound's scabby surface lies a brokenness between us and our own Creator. Left unattended, the wound can result in a total systems shutdown.

Faced with the daunting task of protecting us from the wound, the survival instinct will typically move us in two directions. Our brokenness and separation might drive us toward success. In order to cover the wound, we may strive to dream, become educated, and work harder than we ever knew we could. It might also inspire us to seek love. If we fall deeply enough in love, maybe we could believe the wound is gone forever.

Or, the survival instinct might move us toward spirituality. Even if we keep the wound at bay, we eventually discover we're not good enough. Sooner or later we come to understand that this wound is undeniably bigger than we are. Despite our best efforts, the wound has a nasty habit of showing up uninvited and unexpected. In the midst of a room full of friends, we can suddenly feel alone; surrounded by wealth and success we can feel homeless, insecure, and unsafe.

For many of us, the knowledge of our ultimate inability to fix the wound becomes the doorway to spirituality. Whether our guilt results from a specific tragic event or resembles the gnawing emptiness of Howard Beale, the door opens when we realize that our only real help must come from something bigger than ourselves.

How Does Spirituality Work?

Our spiritual journey begins long before we're ever aware of it. Just as we search for meaning in all the events of our life, we start looking to give meaning to the wound at a very early age. We listen to how others react to stress and pain. We listen for comments about God, religion, and faith. If we finally try to be active in this process, somewhere along the way we might recognize it as our spiritual journey. But even if we don't, it will continue every day of our life with or without our participation.

So what purpose does spirituality serve in our lives? It redefines the meaning of adaptation. It strives to accomplish what centuries of political ambitions, technological advances, humanitarian acts, even evolutionary progress couldn't. Spirituality levels the playing field.

Instead of burning up our lives with the hopeless task of trying to adapt physically to our *external* environment, we adapt spiritually to our *internal* environment. If we make the right connection, we'll have peace, safety, and serenity *inside* of us, and we'll bring it with us wherever we go.

What does it mean to adapt internally? How do we go about adjusting our inner senses?

Unlocking the Door to Spirituality

Like any other survival-driven process, spirituality is an adaptation strategy. Once it helps us accurately *diagnose* a threat, we can take *appropriate* action to meet our specific needs.

The ground rules for successful spirituality are very basic: We have to know what we already believe and why it isn't working. We must identify why we're not already adapted—what are we missing? What is the nature of the threat? What stands between us and the kind of relationship we want with our Creator?

Accurate diagnosis unlocks the door to true spirituality. It provides reasons why one path isn't bringing peace and fulfillment and invites us to choose another.

Spirituality may be our greatest hope for healing the wound and working successfully through our grief, but it's also enormously risky. Diagnosis requires visiting the dark dungeons inside us where our most threatening secrets live. If we stored something there for safe-keeping—even years ago—we're likely to meet it face to face again.

By stripping away the pretense and obligations and fears with brutal honesty, we can confront the real brokenness between us and our Creator. But in our moments of truth, we're deathly afraid of discovering that our separation is permanent and irreparable. We're terrified of finding that our disconnection from God is complete and total.

If we are brutally honest, if we strip away all the pretense and obligations and fears, and confront the real brokenness between ourselves and our Creator, we're deathly afraid that we might uncover a problem for which there is no cure. The deepest of all human fears is discovering that we have a permanent, uncurable disconnection from God.

Now we can really begin to understand why spirituality so often lets us down. Instead of focusing on the source of the disconnection so we can repair it, most of us look for another circuit between God and us. We shop for paths with authority, and trust endorsements from people we admire, including friends and celebrities.

Then we follow this circuit by practicing disciplines of a new school of thought. We believe if we attend enough seminars, hear enough sermons, read enough books, listen to enough testimonials, then we'll finally connect with God. We hold the new vision until we discover this circuit disconnects at the same place as our last.

* * * * * * * * *

If the self-help movement understands the need for spirituality but not the need for guidance, and if the New Age understands the need for guidance but not the source of disconnection, can we look to the church to help us heal our grief?

CHAPTER 9

Beyond Atonement

> My God, my God, Why have you forsaken me?
>
> *—Jesus Christ*

It was a horrible sight. A dying man had nails in his hands and feet, and a crown of thorns on his head. Only a handful of the faithful traveled with him all the way to the foot of the cross. The rest of the followers had fled or were watching with morbid curiosity from a safe distance. No doubt the sharpest pain of all was the loneliness.

As the story goes, the sky turned black and the temple curtain tore in two. The last words he mumbled were simply, "It is finished." Ever since that moment, believers and nonbelievers alike have been trying to understand what he might have meant.

From the beginning there was a mad scramble to make sense of his death. To the Jewish authorities and their Roman coconspirators, the crucifixion was a just reward for bucking the system. To his followers, the death of their leader was a humiliating defeat. A crucified messiah, after all, is something of a contradiction.

Although a cloud of uncertainty surrounded Jesus' death, His life clearly impacted many followers. His teachings and miracles gave people reason to hope, to dream, and to believe in themselves and the wild possibility of building a new world. In the process, they discovered each other learning how to love.

During Jesus' life, many of his followers formed communities of faith. By sharing everything and taking care of one another, they found a sense of belonging and purpose they never knew before. They were finally building the kinds of relationships they had yearned for. But when Jesus died, they faced the probability of losing everything they'd built.

Early Christian leaders faced a monumental challenge. To preserve the unity of the movement and the relationships of their followers, they had to arrive at an understanding of Jesus' death. Diversity among believers further complicated their task.

Romans, Jews, Greeks, pagans, each experienced Jesus differently and then interpreted their experience in a wide variety of ways. To some, He was a healer; to others, a prophet. Others swore He was a political revolutionary.

What could possibly have the power to bind together such a diverse group? How could they keep the dream alive now that their messiah had been crucified?

Their solution was so powerful and ingenious, it gave birth to a religious faith that eventually became one of the most influential forces in history. The death of Christ, they argued, was not an end at all, but a new beginning. As part of God's divine plan, Jesus was more valuable to them dead than alive. Jesus' death reconciled God and humankind.

How could believers arrive at a conclusion that seemed so contradictory to centuries of messianic prediction? Wasn't the promised messiah supposed to reclaim the throne as king, overthrow oppressors, and give back to God's chosen people their homeland and their dignity?

History tells us none of that happened. The long-awaited messiah did not reclaim the throne; He died on a cross. Yet the death of Jesus has been understood ever since to have a miraculous power to connect people to God. Why? Because of something called "theology."

What Is Theology?

Theology has acquired a reputation as a stuffy, lifeless, mostly useless academic subject pursued by pious clerics who mumble their God-speak to each other behind seminary walls. Then they write books that nobody reads.

To some extent this may be true, but it hasn't always been that way. Theology can and should be a work of art.

The word "theology" means the study of God which is, of course, a misnomer because we can't really study God. We study people and their relationship with God, along with the metaphors and stories which are supposed to help us lead more spiritual lives.

Throughout history, the function of theology has remained the same—to connect people to God. The form theology has taken, however, has varied greatly. The form and function of Christian theology has its roots in the Old Testament, where theology was first expressed through ritual sacrifice.

In order to understand the power and genius of what early Christian theology accomplished, we need to take a look back into the history of Judaism and examine the important role sacrifice played in people's lives, binding together their communities and connecting them to God.

Although what are believed to be more civilized forms of worship have long since replaced ritual sacrifice, faint memories of the beating drum, chanting voices, and wafting incense have somehow survived the onslaughts of modernity. In unsuspecting moments, they can still linger in our subconscious.

Sacrifice

We cannot trace the exact origin of religious sacrifice or fully unravel the psychological complexities of believing that the pain, suffering, and death of an innocent victim somehow increase our own well-being. But we do know that ritualizing this emotional mechanism is at the very heart of our Judeo-Christian heritage.

The gory details of animal sacrifice appear in myriad of anthropology and history books. For our purposes, we need only mention that the animal, usually a bull or a lamb, was young and healthy, pure and undefiled. Most important, it had to be the best the worshiper could afford.

In Jewish tradition, the faithful brought their animals to the priest, who had complete authority in all sacrificial matters. The priest slaughtered the animal and sprinkled the blood in various ceremonial ways.

Sacrificial rituals in Judaism were diverse and varied not only in form but also in motivation and significance. While some practices were strictly related to holiday observances, a number of common sacrifices that developed over time were designed to help families and communities invite the "holy" into everyday life. Differing slightly in form, yet identical in function (connection to God), they included:

- Propitiary—a gift presented when seeking favors from God.

- Tributary—an acknowledgment that the deity is entitled to a certain portion of the harvest.

- Votive—a vow or a covenant.

- Freewill—a spontaneous gift.

The priest played a critical role in community life. When culture and tradition dictated a specific seasonal observance, the priest presided over the sacrifice as liturgist, organizing and administering the ritual as God's representative.

In this way the priest might gather the community to express thanks for the harvest, ask for fertility, commemorate the birth of a child, or seek protection before going into battle. Sacralizing the cycles of life through the power of ritual brought people together, strengthened community bonds, and reminded them they were in God's care.

These feasts and rituals were welcome breaks from the brutally hard, often dangerous lives these people led. It was critical that the priest perform these rituals with a deep appreciation for tradition as well as a good measure of individual style and grace. Done correctly, the seasonal celebrations successfully brought the people to the sacred.

The rest of the year the priest faced a different challenge: He had to find a way to bring the sacred to the people using personalized sacrifice to help them overcome disconnection from God and reestablish meaning, hope, even holiness in everyday life. By choosing appropriate sacrifices, he helped his people reconnect with God and broadened his spiritual role. He became a diagnostician. This shift gave birth to theology.

Form and Function

Disconnection from God, then as now, could be generated not only by disobedience, but also by many different kinds of circumstances: a sick child, military conflict, drought, crop failure, death of a loved one.Early Christians believed that each circumstance required a specific sacrificial remedy. They didn't consider finding a remedy for spiritual brokenness a luxury or nicety. It meant survival because disconnection with God threatened their individual, family, and cultural stability.

In each situation, the priest strove to bring the person back to the presence of God through ritual sacrifice. Only the form of sacrifice varied to satisfy individual circumstances. Because the priest diagnosed the situation and ordered the appropriate sacrificial remedy, his diagnosis formed the foundation of his credibility and authority.

The children of Israel experienced many periods of growth and prosperity. During these times they were a shining example to the world of how God can work wonders in people's lives. But facing a series of tragedies—wars, pestilence, famine, and corruption—led the Israelites to ask some very difficult questions: "Where is God in all of this? If we are His chosen people, why are these things happening?" These questions suggested a devastating separation from God expressed with a bitter eloquence in many of the Psalms: "Why have you forsaken your people, Oh God?"

Crises jeopardized the Israelites' individual, family, and community safety and threatened their identity as a people. Dead silence replaced the fellowship they once enjoyed with God. To appease God, the Israelites repented. Through sacrifice, they covered their sins with blood.

The Israelites came to believe that the reason for their separation from God was disobedience. Their solution to this problem, the mechanism for reconnection, they concluded, was sacrifice: God is angry because we have offended his righteousness; He cannot be in relationship with us until we repent and the sin is covered with blood. This theology of reconciliation by sacrifice came to be known as atonement, meaning "at-one-ment."

A whole elaborate sacrificial system quickly rose around the theology of atonement, culminating in a yearly Day of Atonement observance. This solemn occasion included a variety of sacrifices for the priesthood and the people—even a "scapegoat" ceremony whereby all the sins were placed on the back of an unsuspecting goat who was then run out of town.

Atonement offered a powerfully effective solution for guilt. We all make mistakes. We hurt each other, we disobey commandments from God even when we know we are wrong. Guilt can cause a huge rift in our relationship with God. Being able to confess our sins and know they are forgiven can create healing and reconciliation.

Atonement soon became the preeminent theological expression for the children of Israel, the only method for connecting with God. When Jesus of Nazareth was crucified, it was no surprise that Jewish theologians so convinced of the universal importance of atonement would find this meaning in the cross.

New Testament Theology

In the Old Testament, the function of sacrifice—connection to God—remained constant, while forms of sacrifice differed, as needed, in order to ensure the connection. Early Old Testament theology showed real genius. It kept the function of sacrifice—connection to God—a constant. To sustain the connection, they changed forms of sacrifice as needed.

In the New Testament, the crucifixion of Jesus became the "final form" of sacrifice. By fixing form of sacrifice as constant and complete, New Testament theologians faced a radically different challenge from their Old Testament counterparts.

If the cross of Jesus represents the final, complete demonstration of God's love and acceptance of the human race, but the flexibility of changing forms was no longer a creative option for ensuring connection to God, then how would Christian theology support individuals' search for that connection? By shifting focus from the evolution of form to the evolution of meaning, what would be the task of Christian theology?

Through several historical periods, theologians have used a variety of language and imagery to give meaning to Jesus' crucifixion.

The Patristic Period

The conclusions of the patristic period exerted a huge influence over Christianity for more than a thousand years. The major patristic figure was Iraneus (130-200 AD), who spoke of Jesus as the "second Adam," living a perfect life on our behalf. The death of Jesus on the cross, said Iraneus, provided a ransom, wrestling humankind free from the grasp of the devil. We were once "slaves to sin"; now our freedom has been *purchased* through Jesus's blood.

Other theologies of the period basically modified Iraneus' teachings. For example, Tertullian, and Clement of Alexandria, both argued the ransom was paid to the devil instead of to God.

St. Augustine (350-430 AD) is credited with coining some of the theological language still in use today: "the fall," "original sin," and "justification." He also had a vivid imagination with metaphors arguing that the cross was actually "a mousetrap baited with Jesus' blood, luring the devil."

Not to be outdone, Gregory of Nyssa (330-395 AD) introduced the notion that hiding someplace inside of Jesus was a fishhook that God put there to snare the devil. Later John of Damascus broadened the theological understanding of what was accomplished on the cross to include a lengthy discussion on immortality. He argued that through the cross God destroyed death.

With times changing, the world expanding, and the stampede of Crusaders marching across the known world determined to correct the disobedience of nonbelievers, scholars of the medieval period attempted to outdo Augustine by building a "better mousetrap."

The Medieval Period

St. Anselm of Canterbury (1033-1109) focused his theology on the concept of justice. We owe God complete obedience because sin robbed the Creator of the honor which is His due. His holy nature demands some kind of retribution and satisfaction. Punishment is mandatory.

Abelard (1079-1142) took a much different tack. He pointed to the fact that the cross is such a heart-rending demonstration of God's love it *automatically* elicits our love in return.

Thomas Aquinas (1225-1274) wrote what is considered to be the most comprehensive synthesis of what had been said before him, emphasizing that Jesus was our substitute.

Even if we continue reading history to include the writings of theologians such as Jonathan Edwards, Karl Barth, Schleirmacher, etc., we find that after more than 1600 years, Christian theological metaphors may have changed from mousetrap to fishhook to "God-consciousness," but the basic framework has resisted any real modifications. God is pictured as a righteous king, and we are His recalcitrant servants. Because we have sinned and dishonored Him, God demands justice. We must pay for our mistakes. Mercifully, God chose his son, Jesus, to be our substitute and take upon Himself the sins of the world.

But the obvious and dangerous question still remains: *Does the theology of atonement really connect people to God?* Are we surrounded by shining examples of people who have confessed their sins, received forgiveness, and now live in harmony with their Creator?

Unfinished Business

In both Old and New Testament times, the goal of atonement was to give people a consistent, long-term relationship with God. Did it succeed?

The Israelites gave atonement preeminence in the life of their community. Nonetheless, the Old Testament is still very much the story of a people estranged from God. Their spiritual journey continued to be hazardous and broken, one step forward and two steps back. The wars and internal corruption continued. They were conquered and subjugated. God sent prophets telling them to repent, but they resisted. If atonement were meant to help sustain a long-term relationship with God, it had mixed results, at best.

Atonement in Christian history has a similar record. Over the last 2000 years, the Christian church has experienced endless cycles of renewal, prosperity, and collapse.

With such a questionable track record, why is atonement so fiercely protected, not as merely a theology but as the orthodox loyalty test and password for entrance into the "kingdom"? How do we account for the longevity of the theology of atonement? What does atonement accomplish that we're not talking about?

The preeminence of atonement can't be adequately explained by its ability to connect people with God because that has proven to be inconsistent and incomplete. Indeed, atonement may accomplish two other important functions in the life of a religious community. The first one has to do with the priesthood.

With atonement as the only option for reconciliation, a priest has to urge his people to see sin in all of life's traumas, even those that don't seem even remotely connected to disobedience. For example, if a baby dies at birth, the parents must have sinned. If the crops fail, if a storm kills the cattle, if the neighboring army run off with the women and children, it is all because of sin. Atonement requires guilt in order to succeed, even where there is none.

Atonement relieved the priesthood of much of its diagnostic responsibilities. Ironically, in so doing, it greatly increased the priest's power and authority. Now the guesswork was taken out of sacrifice. If all separation from God is the result of sin, the appropriate remedy is *always* atonement. If the completed sacrificial ritual didn't produce the desired reconciliation, it was the believer's fault. He must have failed to confess a secret sin. Institutionalizing atonement created a kind of cushy, diplomatic immunity for the priesthood.

One other explanation clarifies why atonement sustained its power in these communities. Priests could not own land or cattle. While theoretically smoke of a burnt offering might create a soothing incense to an angry God and sprinkled blood might absolve sins, practically the sacrificial meat was the primary source of sustenance for the priest and his family.

Perhaps this explains why priests defended atonement so staunchly. Any consideration of alternate paths to God threatened their power, authority, even their livelihood.

Who Will Save Us from Our Innocence?

Atonement may work very well for guilt, but what happens when guilt is not the issue? What about all those other emotions we can have? What if we're angry, broken-hearted, or frustrated? What if we've done our best, prayed and prayed, but all we hear is silence? What if we're separated from God because we're *innocent*?

I wonder if this is why, not only the Israelites but also religious people throughout history have had so much trouble repenting. When we don't come to the altar hat in hand as quickly as we're supposed to, we're accused of being stubborn and self-centered. But might we have a far more legitimate reason for not seeking atonement?

It isn't because we never feel guilt. We do. We're all sinners. We do things to hurt ourselves and each other. But we have other emotions, too. From the bottom of our hearts, we may feel separated from God for reasons other than guilt. But if we're told the only entrance into God's presence is through the door of repentance and atonement, could it be that some of us simply can't force from our hearts that depth of self-betrayal? If some level of dishonesty has to be part of repentance, can it ever result in true reconciliation?

Even though their livelihood no longer hinges on it, priests and ministers still preach atonement as the only method of reconciliation with God. The church still argues that God expressed divine righteousness by demanding blood sacrifice for human error—even though such behavior on our part would correctly be seen as madness. Then we are told we must love this God. Although the idea of atoning for one's sins carries enough logic to have kept the theory alive all these years, it still holds one fundamental flaw: It lays the responsibility for all the world's pain and suffering at our feet.

If we try to be honest about our other reasons for separation, the church dismisses these issues the same way the Old Testament priest did. We are told that our feelings are really just another form of sin requiring an additional act of repentance. Why doesn't the Christian church understand that while our guilt may be hurting us, our innocence is killing us?

When I first walked into my pastor's office many years ago and told him I wanted to enter the ministry, I got some advice I have never forgotten. He said, "I want you to realize that, as a minister, you will discover there is far more evil in this world than you ever imagined."

He was wrong.

I discovered over the years that there is far more good than I ever imagined. That people hurt each other shouldn't come as a surprise. That there is crime and drug abuse, violence and war is predictable in a world such as ours. What surprises me are the countless acts of love I have witnessed. I have seen a man take off his coat and give it to a beggar. I've seen mothers work two jobs to support their children after the husband ran off with another woman. I know the son of an alcoholic father who was terribly abused and neglected as a child and yet when the father needed care, the son took him into his home and nursed the man until he died. We have all been amazed at the acts of heroism and self-sacrifice that surrounded Ground Zero. It's the good, the innocence, that's really surprising.

There is innocence in this world, lots of it. The most egregious and lasting separations from God doesn't result from guilt. It surfaces when feelings of unfairness, abandonment, and anger rise in the face of innocent suffering.

Although the idea of atoning for one's sins carries enough logic to have kept the theory alive all these years, it still holds one fundamental flaw: it lays the responsibility for all the world's pain at our feet. We're the problem. God maintains His status as perfect, lovable, and just. The alternative to this belief is concluding that God is a monster, deaf to human suffering. That belief is just too terrifying even to consider.

Atonement may have mixed results in its efforts at redeeming people, but it has been very effective at redeeming God.

Beyond Atonement

The cross was given to us by God as a means of connection, an eternal reminder that God is always willing to do whatever it takes, in every generation, to create reconciliation. The function of the cross—its *purpose*—was to prove to us beyond our deepest doubts that God loves us, understands us, accepts us the way we are, and wants us in harmony with Him.

The Church has been charged with the task of helping this God-given event speak, loud and clear, the language of salvation. But the church has forgotten that no particular theological interpretation is inherently sacred. *The value, the truth, the sacredness of any theological meaning given the cross can only be measured in terms of its ability to help people connect to God.*

Atonement is a necessary part of connection to God because guilt is always an obstacle to spiritual wholeness. But atonement alone has never been enough to carry the full weight of reconciliation. The Book of Acts and the letters of St. Paul indicate that, even at the birth of the Christian church, healing, spiritual gifts, and the promise of eternal life were central components in the process of individual conversion and the evangelization of the known world. Throughout Christian history, believers have always required something more than forgiveness to initiate connection with God and, more importantly, to sustain it over time.

Jesus experienced this truth first hand. The crowds that followed Him were not seeking forgiveness, they wanted His teaching and His miracles. The healing of the paraplegic recorded in the Gospels illustrates this point very well. When friends of this crippled man heard that Jesus was preaching in a nearby home, they carried the man past the crowds, pulled him onto the roof, and lowered him into the house with ropes.

Jesus took pity on the man, but His response was a curious one. He looked at the twisted, gnarled man lying on the stretcher and said, "Your sins are forgiven."

There is no greater moment of silence in the gospels than the one that followed that pronouncement because somewhere in that cripple's eyes was the question each of us would ask of God: "After all my years of hoping and praying, don't you know me well enough to realize what I really need?" Jesus yelled out, "Take up your bed and walk!" Forgiveness alone could never have saved this man.

Forgiveness alone can't save you or me, either. In a similar way, each of us comes to God seeking a miracle beyond atonement. For some of us, like the man in the story, it may be some kind of healing. Others seek the promise of heaven when we die. Some seek spiritual powers in the here and now that we hope will prove the presence of God and silence our doubts.

Underneath these individual longings is a more basic and common miracle we all long for—we want to be understood by God. We don't want to be told how we should feel. We want some kind of assurance that God really knows what hurts. We want to know that God understands what it's like to be us. If indeed Jesus was both man and God, then, as the old saying goes, He learned at least one important lesson: It's far more difficult to be a good person than it is to be God.

Salvation from sin and guilt is dangerously incomplete. If God really loved us, wouldn't the cross that caused Him so much suffering and pain be strong enough to hold not just our guilt but our anger as well? Does God not understand that the most difficult separations we feel are because of our innocence?

CHAPTER 10

Unspeakable

A heavier task could not have been imposed
Than I to speak my griefs unspeakable.

—*William Shakespeare*

I had been looking for something new to heal my pain, something new to believe in. Instead, I found something old.

I discovered there is a miracle waiting for those who grieve. This miracle melts away the anger, binds the wound, and shows us beyond the shadow of a doubt that God truly loves us more than we ever imagined.

* * * * * * * * * *

Early one Saturday morning, I was startled when the phone rang in my church office. For the last hour, all I'd heard were the old sanctuary creaking beyond my office door and pigeons cooing outside my window. I was trying to write.

When I heard my mother's voice on the phone, I knew what she was going to say: "Dad passed away last night, son." Numbed as she was, my mother began talking to me about funeral details and how she didn't much like the pastor at her church. I was only half listening.

As she kept on talking, I remembered when I was a little boy the day my father had let me bury him in the sand on a hot afternoon at Jones Beach. We went down by the shoreline where the fresh foam leaves the sand cold and wet, the kind that feels so good on an August sunburn.

I took great handfuls of the sticky stuff and slathered it all over him, molding and shaping as I went along. We laughed and I kept working at fever pitch until I had him covered up to his neck. I made him into a great sand castle daddy. But then I noticed the tide licking at his feet. Panicking, I worked as fast as I could. But no matter how hard I tried to stop it, my sand castle daddy was drifting out to sea, never to be seen again.

That's what it had been like over the last few years. First the lung infection, then the Alzheimer's, then the pneumonia. In the hospital, then home again, over and over. Death was taking him a piece at a time. It seems that people don't die like they used to. Instead, disease and medical procedures gradually devour us until we finally just disappear.

When I hung up the phone, I collapsed on the floor. My head was spinning. Many times I had rehearsed how I was going to feel when I finally got this phone call. I didn't want to be unprepared. I was going to take a long walk out toward the desert to be alone for a while and then try and pray the prayers I had been practicing. "Dear God, thank you for my dad and all that he meant to me." I promised myself I would look at the bright side, try to be positive. None of that happened.

Something inside of me hurt so bad that I thought my guts were going to spill out onto the floor around me. A dam broke inside me. Feelings that had been building up for a lifetime came pouring out. The burning anger I always kept hidden behind walls of discipline and self-control and fear came out in wild screams and a river of tears.

I will never know whether what happened next was a dream, a prayer, or a vision. I just know that it was as real as anything gets in life.

A voice called my name, at first faintly in the distance and then close as a heartbeat. I looked up through my tears and saw a face. Mostly I remember the piercing yet strangely vulnerable eyes framed by a beard and long hair. They broke my heart.

When He reached toward me I saw in one hand a hammer; in His other hand, some fierce-looking spikes.

"Take them," He said. "I want you to do now what you've always wanted to do."

Shaking, I reached out my hands. Suddenly, we were up on a hill, surrounded by a field of grass. The midday sun was blinding. I looked down. He was lying there on a large wooden cross, the wind blowing strands of hair softly across his face. The hammer and nails were burning in my hands.

"Do it," He said.

He didn't try to hide the fear in His face. His lip twitched. His eyes pleaded.

I thought of Cheryl on that fateful night when I watched her wild, evil dance. I had tried to comfort her, but she pushed me away. Hovering over Him I felt the same words that Cheryl had refused forming involuntarily on my lips. I would ask His forgiveness, put down the hammer, and walk away.

Before I could say a word, my arm moved.

The part of me I'd always smothered struck the first blow. When the nail tore through the flesh in his hands, it turned blood red. Then a lifetime of anger broke loose.

I pounded away like a madman and cursed, "Why did you let him suffer! Goddam you for the pain he went through!" Pounding, pounding pounding..." How dare you let him be humiliated that way!"

My hammer hit the nails with a deafening crash. "This is for every hurt and pain this world has ever felt. This is for every crack baby, for every child whose belly is swollen from starvation, for every family ravaged by booze, for every wife who has ever felt the sting of her husband's hand across her face. Goddam it, how can you turn your back on all the suffering in this world! Goddam it, I hate you, I hate you, I hate you!"

His head was turned the other way. Between blows, He looked at me in anguish. I pounded away until I could pound no more. I felt His blood on my hands, on my face. Finally I collapsed. In a raw whisper, He said, "It is finished."

I fully expected to die. I believed that this unspeakable blasphemy would be the end of me. But when I finally awoke, I found myself not in hell, but lying in His arms. He looked at me with the most amazing love I have ever seen and asked, "Now can you love Me?"

****

That was nearly fifteen years ago. Since then, my anger and grief left and never returned. The peace I found that day still remains.

CHAPTER 11

There Isn't a Moment to Lose

"Dance, then, wherever you may be.
I am the lord of the dance," said He.
—*Sydney Carter, from "Lord of the Dance"*

She had awakened me from a trance. Perhaps she thought I was lost. Maybe I just looked lonely. Whatever her motivation might have been, I nearly jumped out of my skin when she gently touched my arm and asked, "Is something wrong?"

I had been crying, the kind of crying self-conscious people like me do. We try to pretend the something in our eye isn't a tear, and the curling, quivering of our lips is just a nervous tick or the beginnings of a sneeze.

She had seen through the awkward mask I was wearing. Seeing through masks was part of her job.

When my eyes finally focused, I saw that the inquisitive voice and gentle hand belonged to a Catholic nun.

Until that moment I had never had any contact with nuns. I learned right away that when a nun puts her hand on your arm, she'll leave it there until she's good and ready to take it off.

Her name was Sister Maria. We met, quite by accident, in a hospital late one afternoon on a rather dreary and otherwise uneventful February day.

There to visit a man who had just undergone multi-bypass heart surgery, I found him in recovery, looking very pale and bionic, attached to all those pipes and tubes and wires and machines that go beep. His eyes were glazed, and a huge bandage covered his chest. The ventilator was breathing for him with a raspy, guttural moan, reminiscent of Darth Vader.

He was an older man, well into his 70s. Because of his age and even more because of his attitude, the whole scene lacked any real urgency. He told me before the operation that he had already lived longer than he had planned so he had little preference as to the outcome. His family felt that way too, which complicated my visit with them in the surgery waiting area. What do you say when nobody cares?

I sat down with the family for a half hour or so and heard overwhelming anxieties and complaints about the doctors, nurses, the courtesy coffee pot's cold coffee, as well as the usual kind of remarks about $10 aspirins and $200 bedpans.

Then they started in on the relatives.

"So and so from Des Moines never cared a lick about anybody but herself and wouldn't lend Mother Theresa a quarter to make a phone call."

"If that granddaughter from Portland thinks a once-a-year Christmas card will get her a mention in the will, why, she's got another thing coming."

Some very candid remarks about the patient followed. One by one, family members rose against the tide of popular opinion which had painted their loved one as a "son-of-a-bitch." In truth, they insisted, he was a nice guy—at least some of the time. It was just that he, like many of us, wished he could have done something different, something better with his life. Maybe then he wouldn't have been so angry all the time.

Although I didn't mention it to the family, it sounded to me like the fellow I just saw in the recovery room had, in reality, been dead for many years. Surviving the multi-bypass wouldn't change any of that.

"Let's all hope for the best," seemed like the diplomatic thing to say. The wife, apparently numb, didn't bother to raise her stare from her Styrofoam cup of cold coffee as I turned and headed in the direction of what I hoped was the parking lot.

I call it "hospital blur." The symptoms are a mental disorientation brought on by look-alike corridors and the sting of Lysol in the nose. The result: while trying to find the way to the parking lot, I got caught like a rat in a maze.

Down many corridors, it all looked the same—odd numbers on the left, even on the right. Every once in a while the colors changed ever so slightly which, to an informed observer, indicated something important, I'm sure. Mainly, however, the hallway just led me forward and I was on automatic pilot until a dramatic change in the scenery stopped me dead in my tracks.

On the wall straight ahead was Mickey Mouse—a medium-sized Mickey with a dazzling, toothy smile. His right arm was extended; his white-gloved hand urged me to turn left. Underneath Mickey a sign in capital letters read, "WE LOVE CHILDREN."

I don't know how to explain why I turned toward the children's wing, other than to say my actions were less the product of better judgments than they were, say, an act of surrender. I could have gone the opposite way and ignored Mickey, but something made me go toward the kids.

Just a few steps forward and suddenly I was awash in a sea of bright colors, an explosive contrast to the bleached white or milky pastel walls coating the other parts of the hospital. The nurses' station was decorated with a variety of teddy bears, some metallic-looking balloons, and a Storytime Big Bird sitting on the edge of the counter, staring off into space with his big, droopy eyes.

"Do you have the one about Big Bird visiting his grandma at the seashore?" I asked, trying to break the ice.

The nurse behind the counter, obviously with time on her hands, launched into an explanation about how this particular Big Bird had recently gone mute because "the thing inside of him that makes him talk is jammed."

She also said they'd given up trying to fix him because one day when maintenance had shown up at the request of the head nurse and had him torn in pieces trying to find out what was wrong, one of the younger kids saw Big Bird dismembered and almost had a heart attack.

"Which way to the parking lot?" I asked.

It was a week or so after Valentine's Day, and I got distracted by the pudgy cupids with their broken arrows still lingering on the wall behind her. When she finished giving me directions, I had to admit I hadn't heard a word she said.

"I'm sorry, would you mind..."

Slowly but firmly she repeated: "Elevator number three. Down to the ground floor, turn left. Follow the hall to the end, then turn right."

Such efficiency. She must have given those directions a thousand times.

"The Cupids stay up all year," she said with a smile.

Her directions were quite accurate, but they weren't complete. The nurse should have warned me about the picture window.

About 25 feet from the nurses station I stopped at a big picture window. As I peered through, I initially thought I was looking at one of those "what's-wrong-with-this-picture" drawings that deliberately blend mistakes into the image.

Children love this game. Usually they find horses sitting in the clouds, ducks on roller skates, fish wearing sneakers, bicycles with no handle bars—anything for a laugh. What I saw through that picture window didn't make sense, but wasn't the least bit funny.

Besides children, the room was filled with things that didn't belong with them. Oxygen tanks, IV tubes, different kinds of electronic monitoring devices contrasted starkly with pictures of the Little Mermaid on the walls and various stuffed members of the Sesame Street Gang on each of the beds.

The children looked wrong, too. Their color was grayish, or grayish-yellow. Most of them didn't have any hair. Their heads were swollen. A haunting blackness surrounded their eyes. Lying in their beds, they all looked very, very sick.

The room was called the Children's Oncology ward, but to me it looked like hell. Standing there, I started to cry.

I felt the hand on my arm. "Is something wrong?" said the gentle voice.

When Sister Maria asked me if I wanted to sit down and talk, all I could do was nod, "Yes."

In a little alcove near the "what's-wrong-with-this-picture" picture window we sat down together. With her hand once again on my arm, the sister asked me which one of the children was mine. That was a harder question to answer than I thought it would be.

"None of them," I answered, but that left many things unsaid.

I told her how I was just wandering around and Mickey told me to come in and have a look. I also told her I was a little sick to my stomach, which was probably the only thing I was sure of at the moment.

Sister Maria was a very old nun. She was also so frightfully thin she seemed to be swimming in her layers of nun's habit. On her face time had painted a mosaic of elegant wrinkles, facial stretch marks, that spoke of a heart that had given birth to a lifetime of love and laughter.

"Why do you hurt so much when you see those children?" she asked. I was getting more than a little uncomfortable and her hand on my arm was an unbearable weight.

"I don't like death," was all I could think of to say.

She pressed on. "I've been working with those kinds of children every day for the last fourteen years."

A little angry with her and suddenly angry at the world in general, I asked, "How can you stand working with death all the time?"

There are moments in our lives, mostly unexpected moments, when something that can only be called grace comes rushing in, and all we can do is stand dumbfounded and hope we don't forget the lesson of the moment. Sister Maria's answer was, for me, one such moment of grace.

She looked at me with her gentle eyes and said these precious words: "I don't work with death." She paused for a moment and then offered a wrinkled smile, "I work with life."

She went on to tell me the different ways she had helped people over the years, in many places throughout the world, in many different capacities. Then she confided in me that, of all the places she had been, there was more life behind that picture window than in any other place she had ever seen.

For a moment I thought she was starting to glow. "It's a different world in that room," she said, "a kind of glorious, magical dance. It's a world where every moment is precious, where nothing is taken for granted. It's a world that has no time for bitterness, anger, or grudges. It's a world where people aren't afraid of their feelings. If they want to laugh, they go ahead and do it, right out loud. If they want to cry, they do that, too. When they cry, they never cry alone; there's always someone to hold them. It's a world where people don't pretend to be something they're not. It's a world where people forgive because life is simply too precious not to. It's a world where people touch and hold each other. It's a world where people take care of each other.

"Once or twice a week, when some of those children have enough strength to get out of bed, do you know what they do with that strength? They get up and go over to the bed of another, to be with someone who is less fortunate. I work with life," she repeated.

Without warning, she got up and extended her hand. Too weak to resist, I allowed Sister Maria to lead me back to the picture window. Time had slipped by. My watch said 5:30. There were some adults in the room now, parents sitting on the edge of the beds. Some were spoon-feeding their loved ones.

Just then one of the children looked our way and waved. A little, shy smile crept across his angelic face. I offered my own shy smile in return and once again I felt that hand on my arm.

"He'd love to meet you," she said.

"Oh, I don't know, I'm late already," I lied.

Without moving her gaze from the window and with just a hint of playfulness in her voice, she said, "What's the matter, are you afraid to fall in love?"

I didn't answer her. I couldn't. I just stared for a long time through the window until the words finally came out. "Do you know the way to the parking lot?"

"Elevator number three, down to the ground floor, turn left, follow the hall to the end, then turn right."

I thanked her, she smiled. I thanked her again, and she just looked back through the window. After a few steps I noticed that just past the picture window was the door I could have gone through. On the door was another cupid.

About a month later I was back in that same hospital. The excuse I used was a woman who had her gall bladder removed, but my real reason was something different. It was that face in the picture window, that very sickly yet angelic face that had smiled at me. I thought about it for a long time, that face in the window. I would go back and visit him. This time I would walk through the door. I even stopped on the way and got him a little toy. Nothing much really, just a wind-up car I bought at a five-and-dime store.

Maybe you know what happened.

"There isn't a moment to lose," Sister Maria had tried to say. Not just on the other side of the picture window, but on our side of the window, too.

Life is too short not to care. It's too short to be afraid to laugh or cry out loud. It's too short to be afraid to fall in love. It's too short to wish you had done something different, something better, with your life. It's too short to be angry.

She was right. It's all too precious, too short, *every* moment. There's a little wind-up car on my desk at home to remind me of that.

Bibliography

Buechner, Frederick. (1992). *Telling Secrets*. San Frasisco, CA: Harper.

Cranston, Maurice. (1991). *The Noble Savage: Jean-Jacques Rousseau 1754-1762*. Chicago, IL: University of Chicago Press.

Dante, Alighieri. (1994). *The Divine Comedy: The Inferno, Purgatorio, and Paradiso (Everyman's Library)*. NY: Alfred A. Knopf.

James, Tad and Woodsmall, Wyatt. (1998). *Time Line Therapy and the Basis of Personality*. Capitola, CA: Meta Publications.

Kübler-Ross, Elisabeth. (1997). *On Death and Dying*. New York, NY: Simon & Schuster.

May, Rollo. (1991). *A Cry for Myth*. New York, NY: W.W. Norton & Company.

Millman, Dan. (2000). *Way of the Peaceful Warrior*. San Diego, CA: H J Kramer.

Peck, M. Scott, M.D. (1998). *The Road Less Traveled*. New York, NY: Simon & Schuster.

Roman, Sanaya. (1989). *Spiritual Growth: Being Your Higher Self*. San Diego, CA: H J Kramer.

Schucman, Helen and Thetford, William, Scribes. (1992). *A Course in Miracles*. Temecula, CA: Foundation for Inner Peace.

Index

ABOUT THE AUTHOR

Herb Orrell, an ordained pastor, has been "hearing things others don't hear" ever since he found his calling in ministry. During his years serving the church, Orrell was often first on the scene,  hearing and seeing what happened before the police were called, before any doctor delivered news, and before individuals had time to gain composure. After seeing, firsthand, the many faces of grief, Orrell decided to share that truth with the world. *Unspeakable* is his story and one that we all share.

Pursuing his calling to the ministry, Orrell completed his undergraduate studies at the University of New Mexico, Albuquerque, and then went on to graduate school at Drew Theological Seminary in Madison, New Jersey.

Upon graduation, Orrell was offered a position with the New York City Council of Churches in the Public Relations Department, but decided instead to accept an appointment as the pastor of a small church in rural New Mexico. For the next 10 years, Orrell served churches of all sizes throughout the Southwest. In 1994, he took a leave of absence from the ministry to write *Unspeakable*.

Orrell lives with his family in Houston, Texas where he works as an author and marketing writer.

Find out more about what Orrell has to say about hope and healing or visit with him online at *http://www.healmygrief.com*.

ORDERING INFORMATION

A GREAT GIFT FOR FRIENDS, FAMILIES, OR LOVED ONES.

Additional copies of **Unspeakable: The Truth About Grief** are available at your favorite local or online bookstore, or directly from the publisher. Orders may be placed by phone, by mail, by FAX, or directly on the web. Purchase orders from institutions are welcome.

❏ *To order by mail:* Complete this order form and mail it (along with check, money order or credit card information) to Bayou Publishing, 2524 Nottingham, Houston, TX 77005-1412.

❏ *To order by phone:* Call (800) 340-2034.

❏ *To order by FAX:* Fill out this order form (including credit card information) and fax to (713) 526-4342.

❏ *To place a secure online order:* Visit http://www.bayoupublishing.com

Name:_____

Address: _____

_____

City: _____ST: ___Zip: _____

Ph:_____

FAX:_____

❏ VISA ❏ MasterCard ❏ American Express

Charge Card #: _____

Expiration Date: _____

Signature:_____

Please send me ____ copies at $24.95 each   _____

Sales Tax 6.25% (Texas residents)   _____

plus $4.00 postage and handling *(per order)* $4.00 _____

Total $ _____

Bayou Publishing
2524 Nottingham, Suite 150 Houston, TX 77005-1412
Ph: (713) 526-4558/ FAX: (713) 526-4342

Orders: (800) 340-2034
http://www.bayoupublishing.com